THEY LOVE YOU, THEY LOVE ME NOT

Vera Katie-Azoory

THEY LOVE YOU, THEY LOVE ME NOT

The Truth About the Family Favorite and Sibling Rivalry

DR. VERA RABIE-AZOORY

HarperCollins*PublishersLtd*

http://www.harpercollins.com

First Edition

Canadian Cataloguing in Publication Data

Rabie-Azoory, Vera
They love you, they love me not : the truth about the family favorite and
sibling rivalry

ISBN 0-00-255426-7

1. Sibling rivalry. 2. Parent and child.
3. Family. I. Title.

BF723.S43R32 1996   306.875   C95-932447-X

95 96 97 98 99 ❖ HC 10 9 8 7 6 5 4 3 2 1

Printed and bound in the United States

This book is dedicated to my father, Daniel Rabie,
who was my Prime Love-Giver,

and

to my daughters, Roxanne and Lisa,
who are my inspiration,

and

to my mother, Hanina,
who continues to fill my life.

Contents

Preface

Work on this book began fourteen years ago, when my younger daughter, Lisa, was only two years old. As the dedication says, the main inspiration for writing it came from watching my own two children, Roxanne and Lisa, interact. As sisters born two years apart, they seemed to begin fighting as soon as Lisa could walk and talk.

Surprised by the lack of literature on sibling rivalry in young children, I began to do my own investigating, and eventually came up with the unique formulations that are proposed herein. You may find it hard to believe it took so much time to come up with these ideas and get them into print. But I'm sure once you read the book you'll agree that the near decade-and-a-half it took to formulate the concepts, invent the language, express the ideas simply and clearly, and answer all the normal questions that come to mind was, in retrospect, really quite short. My only regret comes from the fact that more people couldn't have had access to these innovations, and benefited from them sooner.

At first, my research laboratory was my home. Soon it included the homes of my friends, who diligently tried the recommended techniques on their families and reported their successes and failures back to me. As I gained confidence with the methods, I began to give the same advice to clients in my private practice, meeting with remarkable success. Final confirmation of the theories came from the generous spirit of people who have written their own autobiographies, as well as the writers of the many well-researched biographies of the famous and not-so-famous. Although writing these works may have seemed a self-serving exercise for some of their authors, there is no doubt that these true-to-life works became the reserve data base for this book. My thanks to those who so bravely bared their souls.

I'm sure that readers will find something inside these covers that will enlighten them and change their future in some positive way. I hope it will help change your life, or the life of someone you love.

Acknowledgments

My gratitude to the editors at HarperCollins Canada, Iris Tupholme and Susan Broadhurst, who were astute enough to appreciate the contents of this book, and to Jocelyn Laurence, who helped me write it in simplified form. My thanks especially to June Callwood, who wrote the first ever article about my work on Favoritism in her May 1987 column in the Toronto *Globe and Mail*, which encouraged me to carry on.

Aug. 29/96

THEY LOVE
YOU, THEY
LOVE ME
NOT

Dear Ann,

Thank you for your hard work & contribution to all of society.

Vera Habie-tzoory

1

Introduction

Ann Landers and Abigail Van Buren, née Esther and Pauline Friedman, are identical twins who were treated as two halves of a whole by their loving parents. As children they were inseparable, and passed through most of their life phases, such as puberty and marriage, together. Yet, despite their positions as advisors to the nation on family relationships, they apparently feuded with each other publicly and often. During one eight-year period, they didn't speak to each other at all, and all their reconciliations since then have been only temporary.

No one would argue that these women are not both sharp-witted. They both chose the same profession and are equally successful in it. Yet, according to their unauthorized biography, Esther (Ann Landers) felt overshadowed by her sister, not just throughout their early years, but during her adult life as well. Her marriage to Jules Lederer was hurried, possibly because she was anxious to catch up with her sister, who had had the good fortune to become engaged to a man from an eminent and wealthy family. They had a double wedding. Esther eventually divorced her husband after thirty-six years of marriage.

How is it that sisters and brothers who are raised together in the same environment grow up so different from each other? How do they develop such intense feelings of love and hate—feelings that are likely to stay with them and color the rest of their lives?

Come join me in an adventure in psychology. It will take us on a unique journey of discovery into the human mind, and give you a new and better way of understanding other people's personalities and behavior, as well as your own. You will be able to see clearly how the structure of a family—the relationships between parents and their children, and the relationships between the children themselves—not only has a powerful influence on children's personalities but also affects a good part of their future characteristics as adults.

Most of us have two families in our lives. The first family, known as the *family of origin*, includes our mother and father, as well as brothers and sisters, our *siblings*. Once we marry and become parents ourselves, we form a *family of procreation*. This usually consists of two adults plus the children created from this union.

Everyone would probably agree that their family of origin has been the major force in determining their personality. Our family is central in forming our identity as individuals. Just by looking at your own family of origin, you can see how the patterns of your future behavior were gradually shaped through your life with them.

But how does this actually come about? From a scientific point of view, the family unit has come under serious scrutiny only in the last thirty years. Despite our efforts, we still understand very little about exactly how the family unit works, and most of our attempts at unraveling its secrets have been unsuccessful. This book aims to shed some much-needed light on how the family works, and in so doing, to help you better understand yourself and your own family.

Family Theory and Favoritism

The first chapters of the book address what I have called *Family Theory*. They describe a remarkable, and so far unrecognized, division in the roles that parents assume when they raise their children.

Family Theory holds that parents are *not* created equal. In any family, there will inevitably be a more loving parent (whom I have termed the *Prime Love-Giver*)and a less loving parent (the *Auxiliary Love-Giver*). No value judgment is attached to these roles: it's not necessarily better to be the Prime Love-Giver than the Auxiliary Love-Giver. Both parents have an important part to play in family life. However, every family seems to break down into this division of love's labor.

The book goes on to make the surprising proposal that *Favoritism is a powerful and universal force in family dynamics.* Throughout this book, I use the term *Favoritism* to mean that *parents favor, or prefer, some of their children over others.* This means that *all children are either Favored or, conversely, Disfavored by their parents.* Furthermore, Favoritism—in other words, whether a child is her parents' favorite or not—forms the core of every child's personality development and is the main influence on her future behavior.

To put it another way, Family Theory and Favoritism provides us with two new concepts for analyzing family functioning. Family Theory assigns each parent a role as either Prime or Auxiliary Love-Giver, and treats them as separate but connected contributors to the total pool of love in a family. Favoritism sees children's behavior as a direct response to sibling rivalry, and explains their personality development in terms of whether they are Favored or Disfavored—more loved or less loved—by their parents.

As you read through this book, you will be surprised to discover just how much new light Family Theory and Favoritism sheds on the family. The theory will help you see exactly how the family, the smallest of social units, works to create different personality types by showing Favor toward some children and Disfavor toward others. In short, by understanding the phenomenon of Favoritism, you will gain an unprecedented degree of insight not only into your own life, but into the nature of all humankind.

The Problem with Talking about Favoritism

Over the many years that I have been working on Family Theory and Favoritism, it has become clear to me that parental Favoritism is a hard fact of life. Why has there not been a study of this common and far-reaching phenomenon? Perhaps because even the suggestion that parents favor one child over another is controversial.

One obvious reason is that no loving parent wants to confess to having favorites. Whatever their real feelings, parents believe that they ought not to prefer one child over another. Most people leap to the conclusion that only monsters could be capable of such emotional cruelty toward their children. *Favored* children, for their part, feel embarrassed and guilty about admitting that they were loved more than their siblings, while *Disfavored* children frequently feel that this came about because they are less worthy as people. Almost everyone believes that Favoritism can't involve nice people like themselves or the people they know. After all, they think, only a nasty or dim-witted parent would ever love one child more than another! Consider this example:

> From an early age, Sheila felt she wasn't her parents' favorite child. And she was right. In comparison with her bright and capable older sister, Sheila hardly stood a chance. Her second-best status in the family made her deeply depressed, but she never told anyone about her feelings. Her family just thought she was a quiet, rather sullen child who wasn't much interested in communicating with others. In fact, because of her sense of inadequacy, Sheila would avoid spending time with them. Every evening after dinner, she would hole up in her room, listen to the radio, and read books.
>
> Growing up in the sixties, Sheila learned to label her feelings as an "inferiority complex." When she went to

university, she spent long hours in the library, researching her depression and trying to fathom the cause. At one point in her life, she embarked on a long period of psychotherapy, and was given prescriptions for a wide range of medication. But nothing seemed to get to the root of the problem.

Despite the fact that she hadn't found help for herself, Sheila solemnly vowed that, when she eventually got married, she would *never* repeat her parents' behavior and love one of her children more than the other. However, much to her surprise and dismay, she ended up having two sons who were so different in character that both she and her husband just couldn't help preferring one of them. Sheila wasn't happy at her response to her children, and would lie awake at night and worry, wondering how, given her education and her own childhood experience, she could have let this happen to her.

Favoritism is an explosive topic that needs to be handled with extreme sensitivity. The issue is fraught with conflicting, often painful emotions from parents and children alike. Perhaps because of this, parental Favoritism has consistently been overlooked as a possible source of human motivation. Even in professional circles, very little is known about the impact of Favoritism on people's lives. For almost a century, the study of human behavior has been dominated by Freudian psychoanalysis, and as a result, psychologists have failed to consider the relationship between siblings in general, and Favoritism in particular, as a possible area for serious study and research.

But when I started to review the biographies of a wide selection of famous people, as well as my clinical experience, I found that practically everyone can relate to feeling either Favored or Disfavored. For some, such as French writer Simone de Beauvoir, noted psychological theorist Rudolf Dreikurs, performer Barbra Streisand, and Princess Grace of Monaco, the experience of being a less Favored child left permanent scars. What brought home to me the *universality* of Favoritism, however, was not just reading about famous people, but discovering shortly after the birth of my two children, the existence of Favoritism in my own family. Taking a deeper look at my family of procreation, my family of origin, and also at other families I knew, I began to find it a highly predictable phenomenon.

Think of your own family for a moment. Perhaps you had a sister who was judged the pretty one of the family. Even though you did very well at school—often better than your sister—it never really seemed to count with your parents, who gave your sister most of their praise. Or you might have been the one child in the family who could always get your mother's attention, the one she singled out as special. Or maybe you were the child your father always blamed and punished if you and your brothers got into a fight.

Yet the thought of Favoritism is such an enormous threat to most people that neither the experts nor the general public have been able to acknowledge its prevalence. The simple notion of sibling rivalry is common enough, but thinking of this rivalry as a powerful psychological force has somehow eluded us.

Even if a person finally musters up the courage to mention feelings of being less—or more—loved than a sibling, those experiences are often suppressed or ignored. A father once wrote to me about one of his children: "I think the indications of the root of our son's problem were there all along, staring us in the face, but it wasn't until I read about your work that I saw them for what they are. Our son explicitly told one psychiatrist that we loved our daughter more than him. We just shrugged our shoulders and dismissed the idea as ridiculous."

It's interesting to note that the late Northrop Frye, who became one of the world's leading literary critics, experienced these same feelings, and made the same attempt to ignore them. In excerpts published from Frye's notebooks, he recalls that his mother apparently felt he was "a second-rate substitute" for her first son, who had died in World War I at the age of nineteen. Frye added, "Fortunately I was always too indolent & selfish to make silly efforts about...trying to 'prove' myself..." From the evidence of his life, however, this is quite untrue, since he exerted himself enormously and with phenomenal success in his chosen field. Was he in fact attempting to hide his own deep-rooted feelings of hurt and Disfavor?

In the end, to overlook Favoritism is to miss its significance in understanding both family dynamics and society as a whole. In this book, I propose that Favoritism is a powerful source of human motivation and an inescapable product of family life. Through the course of this book you will come to see that relationships between siblings are of such great importance that in many ways they actually override the parents' influence on the psychological development of their children.

Strange as it may seem to you at this point, once you accept the *universality of Favoritism* and discover that no one can escape it, you can learn to identify its effects, and from there, find it very helpful in identifying and solving problems within either of your families—your birth family, which includes your parents and your brothers and sisters, and your "adult" family, which includes your own children. This book will show that *everyone can identify themselves as either Favored or Disfavored in their family of origin*. At the same time, parents will begin to recognize that *there is always some Favoritism in parental attitudes toward the children in their family of procreation*.

Family Theory and Favoritism offers solid guidance for many of the problems that parents experience with their children, as well as the problems that often pursue people from childhood into their adult lives. I have tried to present my ideas as simply and clearly as possible in order to help you put them into practice in your own life. The concepts I describe will not only make you more aware of the impact your siblings had on your personality but will also lead you to look more closely at the relationships between your children and help explain their behavior. Family Theory and Favoritism provides valuable tools that will allow you to unravel the mystery of the way your children think, feel, reason, and behave, as well as giving you greater insight into your own thoughts and feelings. Most importantly, once you understand the dynamics of Favoritism, you will find yourself in a better position to have a positive influence over your children's personalities and behavior patterns.

Favoritism Throughout Time

Favoritism is a complex phenomenon that is deeply embedded in the roots of our culture. Think of these well-known stories from the Bible:

> Cain and Abel were the first brothers on earth. When both boys made a sacrificial offering to the Lord, Abel's offering was accepted, but Cain's was rejected. Driven by jealousy and rage, Cain murdered his own brother. He then ran away in disgrace, trying to hide his horrible deed from the Almighty.
>
> In another Bible story of two brothers, Jacob's mother Rebecca preferred him to Esau, his twin. In her eagerness to advance the good fortunes of her Favored son, Rebecca convinced the boys' blind father, Isaac, through trickery, to give the sacred birthright to Jacob, the second-born child, even though according to custom, this inheritance belonged to Esau. Contemporary cultural laws dictated that Jacob should not be more privileged, yet in reality he was certainly favored by his mother, who loved him more because of his kind, gentle character. She loved Esau less by comparison because he was a tough and rugged hunter.
>
> As an old man, Jacob was himself dealt a painful blow for showing favor toward his own beloved son Joseph. He stirred up the rage of his ten sons when he fashioned a coat of many colors for Joseph alone. Loving his son as he did, he was grief-stricken when the older boys led him to believe that Joseph had been killed by a desert beast. Yet we can also fully appreciate, as objective readers of this tale, the frustration of the older sons, whose jealousy drove them to hatch a plot to stage their brother's killing in order to be rid of him forever.

Western folklore contains many examples of Favoritism. "Cinderella," for instance, is the classic story of a good-natured and innocent child who suffers unjust discrimination at the hands of her cruel stepmother. "Snow White" is another fairy tale in which a child is punished by her parent for being beautiful and good. Both stories have been popular for many years, and the reason more than likely relates to their universal nature. It is not uncommon for a parent to assign a child Disfavored status simply because the child is viewed as a rival and a threat to the parent. Both "Cinderella" and "Snow White" graphically illustrate how a parent can willfully discriminate against a child who has done nothing to deserve such treatment, as well as showing the anguish that a child in this position must inevitably experience.

The Freudian Legacy

As a woman educated in psychology, I watched my daughters grow up fully expecting to see Freudian theory unfold before my eyes. The girls would fall head over heels in an Oedipal-style love with their father, and by age five, I would surely observe instances of masturbation. At the very least, they would show a keen interest in their lower parts, since their psychic development would be founded on the three fundamental Freudian psychological stages: oral, anal, and genital.

At first merely surprised and then disappointed by the failure of any profound closeness to develop between my husband and the girls, I soon realized that I had been deceived by the theoretical ideas so vehemently taught to me as a psychology student, ideas that I had, until then, swallowed wholeheartedly. What I had learned in school *had not even the remotest connection to what was going on in our daily lives as a family!*

At the time that Sigmund Freud was a student and budding theorist, Alfred Adler and others began to work with the idea that *a large part of personality develops in response to sibling interactions—the natural feelings of rivalry and competition that arise among brothers and sisters.* Interestingly, Freud and Adler were themselves avid competitors. Like rival siblings, each of them sought to dominate the new intellectual arena of human psychology by promoting his own theory of psychological development to the exclusion of the other's.

In the end, Adler's ideas were cleverly debunked by the unrelenting Freud, who advanced the cause of his own theory, which he called psychoanalysis. Phyllis Grosskurth, in her informative book on Freud, *The Secret Ring, Freud's Inner Circle and the Politics of Psychoanalysis*, aptly sizes up the situation when she affirms that "[t]he subtext of psychoanalytic history is the story of how Freud manipulated and influenced his followers and successors."

Unfortunately, much of the primary investigation into sibling relationships, carried out in the early 1900s by Adler, was eventually abandoned. Largely because of Freud's feud with Adler, and any others who dared to oppose him, the only meaningful concept concerning siblings that emerged from their era was *sibling rivalry*. To this day, the notion of rivalry amongst siblings remains the only significant and accepted piece of information that we have on the subject.

As it turns out, dismissing the ideas put forward by Adler and his followers, such as Rudolf Dreikurs, was a great error in terms of analyzing the sources of human behavior. Freudian psychology, based as it is on sexuality, turned the focus of psychology in this century onto the supposed love triangle between Mother, Father, and Child. When we run into trouble with our first child, many of us tend to follow Freud's model of psychoanalysis and search for answers in the relationship between mother, father, and the first child. When difficulties occur with a second child, we use the same approach—mother, father, child— as we do for the third child, and so on. In other words, we tend to analyze our children's behavior or our own family background by looking only at the effect that *parents* have on each child and ignoring the impact of *siblings* on each other.

Because Freud had a massive influence on Western thought, when someone goes to a therapist or psychiatrist for help, the professional rarely delves into *sibling relationships* as a possible source of emotional problems. Sibling rivalry is regarded merely as an unpleasant reality, something that happens to just about everyone and that we all have to endure. The person's feelings about his or her siblings are usually not considered relevant, either to emotional stability or to personality development.

Parents and the "Normal" Family

Sarah consulted her family physician when she had a problem with one of her children. She had five kids, and couldn't understand why this particular child was giving her and her husband such a hard time. Her son was uncooperative, surly and generally bad-tempered, and none of his parents' efforts to talk to him about his behavior or discipline him, had any lasting effect.

Sarah's family doctor referred her to various mental-health practitioners, but none of this seemed to help. At last, Sarah returned to her own doctor, declaring that she was at her wit's end. Despite all her efforts, she found herself in exactly the same predicament as before she'd embarked on the consulting circuit.

In response to her frustration and distress, the doctor reassured her that he himself had frequently counseled families with problem children. Thanks to this experience, he had discovered that, as he put it, "There's always one rotten apple in every barrel." He advised her to accept the situation with her son and just be thankful for the happiness she derived from her other children.

Sarah left the office feeling even more discouraged than before. She was going through a lot of pain over her son, but it was clear that the good doctor had no constructive guidance to offer her. Was there really nothing she could do?

Whatever our educational background, none of us have much information about how the family is supposed to work or about how its members feel towards one another. Even talking about families presents difficulties. What exactly is a "normal" family? Is it "normal" to have one child out of step with the rest, as Sarah did? Certainly, her opinion about this was different from her doctor's. Traditional psychology provides no clear definition of a normal family, although we often hear references to the "dysfunctional" family. A normal family can no longer be defined as a husband, wife, and 2.5 children, since the many permutations and combinations of families that have begun to take shape are all valid versions of normalcy today.

In this book, I use the same broad definition that Western society applies to parental fitness: *A normal family is any family where one or more adults is considered fit to raise the children.* This broad definition is appropriate because the ideas contained in Family Theory and Favoritism can be applied to *every functioning member of society.*

Alongside this generous definition of normalcy runs an extremely important theme that is implicit throughout the book. Despite the fact that the idea of Favoritism might be interpreted as a criticism of parents' behavior, one of my basic premises is *parents' indisputable good intentions.* In all the discussions about Favoritism in this book, I never assume that any parent is either deliberately nasty or simple-minded. Quite the contrary, I automatically presume that most parents are sincerely concerned with their children's welfare. Based on experience and observation, I have found that parents' sincerity—their desire to do their best for their children—is present in the great majority of families, and that most parents are in fact willing to sacrifice a great deal to raise their children well. Excepting the small minority of adults who abuse their children, *I never question parents' overall goodwill toward their children, and I always grant them full credit for good intentions.*

Since most parents start out with the best of intentions when they have families, you might well ask: If we pour all our love and energy into raising our children, why don't they all turn out perfectly? Or, why don't they all turn out the same? Furthermore, if we treat them all equally, why is it that we don't end up loving them all the same way? And why don't they all love us back the same way?

Parents usually try to provide their children with as many comforts as they can afford. It is a sad fact of life, however, that once their children have grown up and left home, many parents have a nagging feeling that their parenting was somehow inadequate. Privately, they are plagued with the knowledge that one or more of their children is dissatisfied, and that the situation is likely to remain that way forever, no matter what they try to do to correct it. It is a problem similar to unrequited love: the unhappy predicament of longing for a loving relationship that will probably never materialize.

Tragically, these family conflicts often remain unresolved and lead to lasting feelings of pain and personal failure, both for the parents and for the children. As parents and guardians of our young, we frequently end up asking ourselves: Is there something we've missed? Can there be part of our child's development that we've failed to understand?

The Role of Heredity

Most parents at one time or another look to *heredity* as a way of understanding their child. Aren't a child's genes responsible for a good part of who he becomes? If a child has a personality that others find unpleasant, why should the parents be blamed? Isn't it possible that some children are simply born less likable, while others are more likable by nature?

Just as a child can inherit physical traits such as blue eyes or ears that stick out, it seems logical to assume that she could inherit emotional or behavioral attributes too. Parents might believe that their retiring son is just like Grandpa George, who was extremely shy, or that their outgoing daughter is the spitting image of Aunt Emma, who has always been very sociable. A rebellious child might be compared with the black sheep of the family, or a child who seems obsessed with money might be linked to a miserly distant cousin who amassed a fortune.

Desperately seeking answers to problems with their children, many people resort to blaming the black box of heredity. One important argument against using heredity as an explanation for personality, however, is that it is just too simple and convenient an excuse. If parents assume that their children's personality traits are inherited, and therefore fixed and unchangeable, they aren't very likely to try to alter them. In fact, the parent may think, "It's too bad that Brian was born with such a terrible temper. He was a crabby, cranky baby from the start, and he never changed. He reminds me of my youngest brother Sam, who was just the same as a kid and who's still pretty irritable. I guess Brian is like his uncle, and there's nothing much I can do about it."

Following the logical course of this train of thought, parents might be tempted to wash their hands of responsibility for their child's behavior. But there is inevitably a backlash to this attitude. If parents dissociate themselves altogether from their child's difficulties, they may end up feeling trapped and victimized by their own children. After all, if heredity is such an immovable and unchangeable force, then parents are forced to passively accept any behavior their child chooses to dish out.

Similarly, adults can write off their own bad behavior to heredity, without having to make the effort to change their ways. "My mother told me I was always difficult, right from the start," Brian might say as an adult. "I can't help losing my temper. I don't mean anything by it. It's just the way I am. Look at Uncle Sam—he's the same way. He gets annoyed at anything. This kind of bad temper seems to run in the male side of our family."

For parents desperate to find solutions to problems with their children, and for adults who have decided to make an honest attempt to control their antisocial behavior, any viable explanation that emphasizes *environmental* rather than hereditary factors—in other words, anything that suggests there *is* something you can do—is worth serious consideration. Concerned adults who can put aside their beliefs about heredity, and instead look seriously at the theory of sibling relations and Favoritism contained in this book, may be surprised to observe the effects that even minor changes in their attitudes can make in their own or their child's behavior. In fact, my experience as a professional and a parent strongly suggests that *most children are born remarkably equal in terms of their personal and intellectual attributes*. The real differences among people lie in the way that these endowments are used. I will return to a more detailed discussion of heredity in Chapter 6.

The Significance of Theory

A final word before we venture into this exciting new realm of human study. Modern society has come to value research very highly. Many people believe that new information should only emerge from research supported by statistics. Indeed, research is a wonderful thing, and needs to be done before we invest our belief in any new doctrine. But all research, to be coherent, needs a theory at its root. Theories guide research, and in order to be meaningful, most research projects should begin with a well-constructed theory.

Traditionally, psychological theories about human development have come from people who have had no direct experience with raising children. Freud developed his theory of psychoanalysis while working with mental patients, and had little time or patience for gathering real, hands-on experience from his own children. Another well-known theorist, the Russian physiological psychologist Ivan Pavlov, examined the body's responses to certain stimulation. He developed what is termed Behavioral Theory by observing a dog salivate reflexively at the sound of a bell. Out of these laboratory observations emerged the popular stimulus-response paradigm, now widely used as the model for human learning. Birth Order Theory, which examines family life and links people's achievements with their birth positions, came out of biographical studies. Although it has little support in reality, this theory's advocates have pursued it for decades.

The only viable theory of human development that has withstood the test of time and rigorous research is that of the French psychologist Jean Piaget, through which he was able to distinguish four stages of a child's intellectual development. Interestingly, Piaget constructed his theory from *the observation of his own children* and their varying styles of learning at different ages.

However, since the erosion of Freudian theory that began decades ago, a comprehensive viewpoint in psychology—one that attempts to explain a large part of human behavior—has been missing. Family Theory and Favoritism represents a breakthrough in this respect. Founded on my observations of family interaction and sibling behavior, as well as on the fact that these same patterns tend to be repeated in most families, it proposes an explanation for *all* personality and human motivation.

By reading this book, you too will learn how to clearly identify these patterns, and will be introduced to a whole new world of psychology. Armed with your new knowledge, you will then have access to more ways to solve family problems than you have ever enjoyed before.

2

The Early Stages of Family Life

Julie and Henry met at work, and when they decided to get married three years later, thought they knew each other fairly well. They took plenty of time to plan their new family and were ecstatic at the arrival of their son, Sean.

Because she was on maternity leave, Julie took on most of the child-care duties. By the time her leave was over, she found it too hard to part with Sean, and insisted on staying home to raise him herself.

Although Henry went along with most of Julie's decisions, he was having a hard time coping with the changes since Sean's arrival. For one thing, his wife was almost always occupied, and even when she did have a bit of time, Sean came first. The home was constantly a mess, meals together had become a rarity, and the family income had dropped substantially.

Worst of all, Henry felt there was a strong, intangible bond of closeness between his wife and his son—one that he just couldn't penetrate. Sean preferred to go to Mommy when he needed comforting, and Julie seemed to have nothing on her mind but Sean: Has he eaten? Is he tired? Is he feeling well? Rather than rock the boat, though,

Henry kept his unhappiness to himself. But he often thought that marriage and child-rearing had not turned out the way he'd expected.

Julie was unhappy too, but for very different reasons. She couldn't understand Henry's lack of tolerance toward Sean or his apparently increasing lack of regard for her. She began to question her relationship with Henry and wondered how wise she'd been to marry a man who, after all, seemed to be quite a selfish person.

An easy way to explain Family Theory is to start with an ordinary couple like Julie and Henry. When a couple lives together or marries, sooner or later frequently follows the birth of a child. And once a baby is born, the adults' roles change. They are no longer just partners or spouses but *parents* to the newborn child.

As soon as a child enters the family, something remarkable happens—something that forms one of the cornerstones of Family Theory. Very early in a child's life, *the child selects one parent to be her main provider of love*. This choice, which is *not* based on the parent's sex, means the child forms a strong emotional attachment with one parent in particular. I call this parent the Prime Love-Giver, or PLG for short. In Julie and Henry's family, Julie had emerged as the Prime Love-Giver for Sean.

The other parent, in this case Henry, who becomes the secondary provider of love for the child, I have named the Auxiliary Love-Giver, or ALG for short.

Like that between Julie and her son Sean, the relationship between the Prime Love-Giver and the first child is intense and almost immediate. They gravitate toward one another like magnets, creating a powerful emotional connection. Normally, the process in which the child assigns his parents their roles as either PLG or ALG, occurs within three to six months after the child is born. The child clings to the Prime Love-Giver, whom he perceives as more loving than his other parent, and the Prime Love-Giver responds by providing the love and nurturing that the child seeks.

From this point onward, a *Circle of Love* is created in the family that includes only the Prime Love-Giver (in our example, Julie) and the child. This Circle of Love becomes the central focus of loving feeling in the family. The parent who, like Henry, takes on the role of the Auxiliary Love-Giver remains outside the Circle of Love and functions in a separate emotional sphere, which I describe in detail in Chapter 3.

A family's Circle of Love, which is formed from the closeness that exists between the Prime Love-Giver and the first child, can be pictured as follows:

$$\left(\begin{array}{c} \text{PLG} \\ + \\ \text{child 1} \end{array}\right) \quad + \quad \text{ALG}$$

Separating parents into two distinct roles—Prime Love-Giver and Auxiliary Love-Giver—to their children, as opposed to the more popularly accepted notion of parents functioning as a cooperative unit, is the essence of Family Theory.

Choosing a Prime Love-Giver

At first, the whole idea of a child choosing only *one* Prime Love-Giving parent, to the partial exclusion of the other parent from the Circle of Love sounds shocking. It means, of course, that the Prime Love-Giver is more emotionally important to the children than the other parent. It also means that the emotional responsibility for the children falls on the shoulders of only one parent. The notion of Prime and Auxiliary Love-Givers clearly contradicts our ideal in which two parents participate equally when they raise their family.

Yet, if you think about it for a moment, you'll realize that in most families—your own or your friends'—it is often no secret that the children depend on one parent in particular for most of their love and nurturing. Family dynamics mysteriously move the family members in this direction. Without talking about it, everyone decides whether to assign prime or auxiliary status to each parent.

Once you're aware of this division of love's labor, it's often easy to spot the way roles have been assigned in other families, including your own. In the case of a family that's familiar to us all, for example—Princess Diana and Prince Charles of England—Diana is obviously the Prime Love-Giver. However much Prince Charles may indeed love his children, it is clear that he plays a secondary, or Auxiliary Love-Giving, role to the young princes, William and Harry.

Acknowledging that each parent plays a separate and different role in the family not only clarifies our view of how the family functions but also provides a badly needed theoretical basis for figuring out how families work. Until now, people have ignored the distinction between parents' roles. We've insisted on clinging to the illusion that both parents play an equal emotional role in their children's lives. This has made it almost impossible to understand family life and its effect on children's personalities. There have been no significant discoveries about the way in which families evolve, nor any workable solutions for the common problems that families face.

But how does a child actually go about choosing a Prime Love-Giver? What criteria does the child use to make this choice? And how can *you* identify whether a parent is a Prime or Auxiliary Love-Giver—in your family of origin, your family of procreation, or even in a friend's family?

In some families it's easy to locate the Prime Love-Giver, while in other families the roles of the two parents may look highly intertwined and evenly balanced. In Chapter 3, I offer a specific set of guidelines that you can use to identify the Prime Love-Giver in almost any family. What follows here are five questions that I am often asked when people begin to wonder about how children choose one parent as their Prime Love-Giver. Some of these criteria are relevant to children when they choose their PLG and some that we may expect to be relevant are not.

1. Does *Love* Affect the Choice of Prime Love-Giver?

Attachment to a single love-giving adult appears to be a fundamental human need that is closely bound up with a child's survival instinct. *Every child seems to be born with a powerful drive to seek out one Prime Love-Giving adult to fill her emotional needs.* The child assesses the amount of love and kindness that she thinks is available from her adult caregivers and, based on this gut feeling, attaches herself to the one person who seems to be most capable of fulfilling these needs.

The kind of love that a Prime Love-Giver supplies is often described very accurately in biographies, even though the phenomenon itself is not formally recognized. For a child, nothing is more important than love in deciding who will be the Prime Love-Giver. Given two parents to choose from, the child selects the Prime Love-Giver by comparing the love provided by each of them. Here is an example from the life of a well-known comedienne:

> Joan Rivers adored her mother, and is proud to inform readers of her autobiography that she took on many of her mother's finest character traits. Her mother apparently had a rigid exterior, but underneath there was a great deal of warmth, compassion, and sensitivity to the needs of other people.
>
> As far as her father was concerned, though, Joan says that she and her sister Barbara saw very little of him, and therefore couldn't really love him. As a doctor, he spent a great deal of time making house calls, even forfeiting holidays and vacation time for the sake of his work. What Joan found most painful of all, however, was that her father was too stingy to allow the family to live well on the money that he did earn.

Joan Rivers' parents are a good example of a clear-cut division between the Prime and Auxiliary Love-Givers. However, the personality differences between parents—in Joan's case, between a sympathetic and loving mother and an absent and miserly father—are not always so apparent. When two parents seem, on the surface, to be more or less equal in terms of how lovingly they behave toward their child, the child's instinct comes into play. This instinct is so well-developed right from the start—thanks to the child's inborn need to survive—that she can make fine distinctions between a little more love and a little less love. Thus, *even if both parents have a great deal of love to offer, a child will usually still choose the one who is even slightly more loving than the other as her PLG.*

How does the child make the often subtle assessment of his parents' ability to provide love? As a general rule, the adults who are best equipped to give their children the love they require, and are therefore most likely to be chosen as Prime Love-Givers, are *those who are able to suppress their own needs in favor of the needs of the child.* They are, in effect, the ones who are more willing to make sacrifices on the child's behalf and who are consistently able to put their own desires after their child's.

A child is extremely sensitive to the normal signs of love: smiles, stroking, affectionate touching, eye contact, casual chatting, intimate conversation, and the like. We are all innately equipped to respond to these expressions of love, but in a child's case, these signs help her pinpoint the source of the most love and affection. Putting together both physical and emotional cues, the child chooses as Prime Love-Giver the parent who seems to be most capable of fulfilling her need for care and affection.

Far from being something that happens by chance then, the search for a Prime Love-Giving adult seems to be something that is programmed into every child's psyche. This gravitation toward one main source of love involves a kind of sixth sense that all children are born with and that they exercise with extreme shrewdness. This acute sensitivity to the most potent source of love is a universal human trait that cuts across factors such as age, sex, race, color, and even intellectual ability. In other words, any child, regardless of his background, has the ability to make this distinction.

It is important to note in passing that assessing parents based on their ability to deliver love applies only to love *directed toward children*. It is associated exclusively with servicing children's needs. Love between adults is of an entirely different quality and origin.

2. Does *Gender* Affect the Choice of Prime Love-Giver?
Who will play the role of Prime Love-Giver for a family—the mother or the father? Does the choice of PLG depend on the gender of a parent? Consider this example:

Dave had been a practising doctor for some time when he met and married Sheryl, a lawyer. A year or so later, they had a daughter, and five years after that, a son. When the boy was two years old, the couple decided to get a divorce, and custody of the children was awarded to the mother. While Dave did not contest the custody order, he felt very attached to his children and was unhappy at being separated from them. Sheryl, on the other hand, seemed less emotionally involved with her son and daughter, even though she had wanted—and won—the right to sole custody.

Sheryl's attitude must have communicated itself to her children. Soon after the divorce, the daughter ran away from her mother's home and went to live with her newly remarried dad. Years later, when the son grew up, he too decided to leave his mother and take up permanent residence with his father and Sheryl did not contest the change. Dave obviously had a great deal of love and warmth to offer the children, and it appears that the choice the children had made in favor of their father, which they had both acted on independently, was a clear statement that they preferred him as their main provider of love.

As I said earlier, sex does *not* determine who becomes the Prime Love-Giver in a family. Given that the choice is based on the amount of love that each adult can give the children, it follows that *gender is not an important factor in this decision.* In contrast with other approaches to family life, *Family Theory places "mothering" and "fathering" on an entirely equal footing.* Both terms give way to "parenting," allowing a parent of either gender to be the Prime or Auxiliary Love-Giver.

In any family, the mother and the father have an *equal* chance of becoming the Prime Love-Giver. This is clearly illustrated in the story above. Dave's children both left their mother's home and returned to their father, despite the court order awarding principal custody to their mother. Clearly, both children felt that their father was their Prime Love-Giver, a pattern that had been set before their parents' divorce. On the other hand, in the story of Julie at the beginning of this chapter, it is equally clear that the mother had assumed this position.

In any family, the parent who is finally chosen as the Prime Love-Giver is simply the one who, according to the children, can provide more warmth and affection than the other, and the one who seems more willing to suppress her or his needs in favor of the child's. It is a comparative exercise carried out by the child and whether the chosen parent happens to be male or female is irrelevant.

The Social Bias

In our society, there is a strong tendency to associate the primary source of love with mothers. We tend to equate "mothering" with nurturing activities such as feeding, providing physical comfort, or giving emotional support. Popular wisdom would have us believe that the so-called mothering instinct is inherent in virtually all women and automatically swings into action as soon as a child is born. No doubt this belief stems from the physical closeness that is inevitable with pregnancy, childbirth, and breastfeeding.

For some time, custody battles were almost always resolved in favor of the mother (though this is now beginning to change), since mothers, because of the social prejudice in their favor, were automatically regarded as the primary caregivers for their children. However, this line of thought is gradually being revealed as the myth that it is. Many women are finally admitting that in fact they lack a mothering instinct and never really felt that surge of desire to care for their newborn child. They have been thrust into the mothering role not only because of their helpless infant's urgent demands but because they feel driven to at least try to comply with the social norm.

There are, of course, many women who truly enjoy being a mother, with all that the role implies, but we must accept the fact that there are at least some who do not. Consider the following example:

Alice, a beautiful girl, had gone into modeling right after high school. After working hard at it for five years, she decided to open her own modeling agency. She loved her work, and was doing very well when she met and married Steve, a photographer.

The day she gave birth to their son, Alice suddenly found herself feeling very sad, an emotion she chalked up to post-partum depression. Like an aspiring Supermom, she planned her baby into her organized lifestyle. She woke up at 5:00 a.m., got herself ready by 5:30, fed and dressed the baby by 6:00, took him to the babysitter by 6:30 and was at work by 7:00. At midday, she pumped her breasts and stored the milk in the fridge for the next day's noon-hour feeding.

Alice's mother-in-law voiced her objection to this hectic lifestyle. "Do your work from home for a few months," she suggested. "Steve can manage the business for a while, and you can look after the baby. Otherwise, you're going to go crazy, and you're going to drive your husband and your kid crazy too." Alice didn't agree. She'd been a career woman all her life, and that was the way she liked it.

In the meantime, Steve, who had a more flexible schedule, was more than happy to make himself available to the child, and found the time to visit the babysitter's home at least once a day.

This pattern continued until a second son was born, when it made sense to hire a nanny. But Alice's attitude toward child-rearing didn't change. She derived enormous satisfaction from her work, while Steve loved participating fully in their sons' lives. Alice continued to take care of the organizational aspects of their life, while Steve fitted his own work around the boys' needs and made sure that everyone was happy.

When it comes to women and "mothering," some may do a good job while others may not. Some may feel they ought to do better, and get depressed when they realize they simply lack the patience. They may feel forced to try to cultivate a talent for caring and nurturing that would never have appealed to them otherwise. After a time, they frequently build up a close emotional bond with their offspring, but this is a secondary emotion, not a primary one.

Family Theory recognizes that the desire to nurture children and provide them with the love they need is something that adults do not experience equally. Some individuals, whether male or female, are more inclined to form close relationships with children than others. Steve liked being involved in his sons' lives more than his wife did; such adults seem to enjoy fulfilling children's needs in exchange for the love and gratification they hope to receive in return. The desire—and the ability—to become a child's primary source of love reflects the nature of the individual adult, and isn't necessarily tied to other factors such as gender or the hormonal changes that go along with childbirth. In any family, whether a parent becomes the Prime or Auxiliary Love-Giver seems to depend most on *the desire of each parent to occupy the role.*

From a Family Theory viewpoint, then, *a father stands as good a chance of becoming a family's Prime Love-Giver as a mother does.* If the father's personality is warmer and more caring than the mother's, the children will sense this, and he will easily slide into the role of PLG. It's true that the *opportunity* for a woman to become a Prime Love-Giver is greater. Her role in giving birth and breastfeeding means she's likely to spend more time caring for her baby, at least initially. However, my personal observation of families suggests that, in practice, fathers become Prime Love-Givers almost as often as mothers. In other words, about half of all households have chosen the father as the Prime Love-Giver, while about half have chosen their mother.

Popular references to "mothering," then, carry with them a gender bias that has serious repercussions. The idea that only mothers can fill this nurturing role places tremendous pressure on women to prove they are more loving than their male counterparts. At the same time, the notion that women are somehow innately better at being loving and warm often discourages men from having a close relationship with their children, when the truth is that they would actually like to be more demonstrative but feel it isn't socially acceptable.

Our belief in the primacy of mothers is so widespread that many women become deeply disappointed, or outright offended, when they learn they are *not* their family's Prime Love-Giver. Often, a woman's female identity is seriously threatened if she sees her mate being the more gentle, affectionate partner, while she assumes the more disciplinarian role in the home. If she is honest with herself, she may in fact be less attached to her children, but she likely feels that if she isn't the main source of love to her children, she has failed not only in her duty as a mother but also in her role as a woman. Such women often respond to this feeling of failure by rejecting the notion of a PLG/ALG split altogether and insisting that in their household, both parents hold equal emotional importance in the children's eyes.

However, women who are not the family's Prime Love-Giver should comfort themselves with the knowledge that the issue in no way reflects on their worth, either as parents or as individuals, and has nothing to do with the success or failure of their family. The division of emotional labor between parents is a perfectly normal but so far undocumented event that happens in all families.

In fact, the potential for *either* parent to assume the role of Prime Love-Giver is good news for both men and women. From a woman's standpoint, once the social pressure to constantly appear soft and loving is lifted from her shoulders, she doesn't need to be saddled with this social expectation or to bear the emotional responsibility of feeling that she *must* be the main source of love for her family. If a woman is naturally inclined to be the family's Prime Love-Giver, she can, of course, happily occupy the role, but there is no social obligation for her to do so.

From a man's point of view, Family Theory paves the way toward recognizing the significant contribution that many men make in bearing the emotional burdens of raising a family. There is still a social bias that surrounds the question of men participating fully in a family, and this means that the role of a father as the PLG is largely unacknowledged. Family Theory allows a man to take on the emotional responsibility for his children if he wishes, without feeling either that he is in some way emasculated or that he is usurping what should more properly be a mother's role. The unrecognized role of the Prime Love-Giving father will be discussed in detail in the final chapter.

3. Does the *Quantity of Time Spent Together* Affect the Choice of Prime Love-Giver?

Parents rarely spend absolutely equal amounts of time with their children. Particularly when a child is young, there is usually one parent who spends more time caring for the infant's immediate needs—feeding, changing diapers, or putting the child to bed. And as the child grows older, one parent usually takes on the bulk of the child-care chores, from taking the child to school and picking her up to making school lunches and supervising homework.

It may seem strange at first, but these daily-care activities don't ultimately decide who is to be the PLG. In other words, the person whom we commonly refer to as the primary caregiver is not necessarily the Prime Love-Giver. The term Prime Love-Giver refers to the quality of the emotional connection between a parent and a child, rather than to the quantity of time spent with the child. Thus, if there are two parents involved in caring for a child, *the sheer amount of time that one parent spends with the child doesn't necessarily indicate that parent's emotional importance to the child.* In the familiar case of the father who goes to work and leaves the mother at home all day with the children, the mother certainly spends far more time with the children than the father does. Yet it is quite possible that the father, not the mother, is the children's Prime Love-Giver.

The following brief description of the early life of Indira Gandhi shows how even a long-distance relationship with a PLG can be valid for a child:

> "Indu" (her pet name) was only four years old when her father (Jawaharlal) and grandfather (Motilal) were taken away from home and put in jail for their beliefs. Indira loved

her father enormously, and felt his loss deeply. When she had to face up to the fact that neither man would be coming home, she was inconsolable. She was not as close to her mother, who was rather young and not highly regarded in the Nehru household, but even this possible source of love was taken away from Indira when her mother, too, was imprisoned for long periods of time.

From her early childhood, Indira's father was highly preoccupied with her education. From his jail cell he sent her instructions about which books to read. During one period of imprisonment, he wrote her many letters about world history, which were later collected into a book and became a literary classic.

As with gender, the only vital requirement for a Prime Love-Giver is that the parent be willing to satisfy the child's need for love and emotional comfort, and *provide this in greater measure than the partner.* The parent who shows more love and caring will usually assume emotional priority, even if this parent spends less time with the children.

Naturally, there must be enough opportunities for a parent and child to establish a loving relationship. A problem could arise if, for example, the parent who would have made the best Prime Love-Giver lives out of town. In this case, the parent simply might not be around for long enough to allow the primary relationship with the child to develop. But given that a child has reasonable contact with both parents, one of them will eventually be chosen as Prime Love-Giver based on whom the child prefers to be with, not on whom the child sees more often.

4. Does *Biological Parenthood* Affect the Choice of Prime Love-Giver?

Family Theory emphasizes the psychological and emotional connection between a Prime Love-Giving parent and a child, which is experienced as their *love* for each other. Given this assumption, *the biological connection between an adult and a child is a relatively minor consideration.* A relationship with an adoptive parent, or another adult who assumes the role of Prime Love-Giver, can provide a child with a perfectly solid and valid emotional connection.

There have been several recent cases of adopted children who, after some time had passed, were reclaimed by their biological parents. Professionals, having little theoretical guidance, have stood by silently and made no comment. According to Family Theory, however, once a child is six months old, he has already begun to form a permanent emotional connection with a Prime Love-Giving adult, and it would therefore be unfair to move the child from his adoptive home, unless there were very good reasons to do so.

5. Do *Other Sources of Love* Affect the Choice of Prime Love-Giver?

Other adults who live in the same household with a family may develop an especially close relationship with a child and provide him with alternate sources of love, even though they aren't the child's parents. Consider the case of Sir Winston Churchill.

> Although Churchill had a privileged upbringing, he rarely saw his mother. His father, whom he idolized as an accomplished orator, was unpredictable and given to fitful rages in which he verbally attacked young Winston in an entirely merciless way.
>
> The biography of Winston Churchill reveals that his greatest source of spontaneous love and warmth was his nanny, Mrs. Everest, whom he called "Womany." It was to her that he confided his innermost feelings and concerns, and who, no doubt, was his prime provider of love, although his deep longing for his real mother, whom he knew only from a distance, never quite left him.
>
> In her later days, when Mrs. Everest was treated badly by the family, Winston went out of his way to try to make her comfortable, and when she died, he mourned her deeply.

According to biographer Piers Brendon, the loss of Mrs. Everest seemed to leave Winston, at twenty-one years old, with a somewhat hardened attitude to life.

We've all seen how valuable additional love can be supplied by a grandparent, a nanny, or even a nurturing older sibling. The grandparent or nanny may be a very caring person who spends a lot of time with the children, and may even significantly increase the whole family's sense of security and emotional stability. However, as long as the child's real parents are around and are willing to participate in the child's upbringing, *an alternate provider of love is not generally chosen as a Prime Love-Giver.* Only if a child's parents are neglectful, physically absent, or merely inaccessible, as were Winston Churchill's, will the child select an alternate PLG.

Nonetheless, the choice of a Prime Love-Giver other than a parent, when the parents are around, is rarely wholly successful. In Churchill's case, his real mother was around and could have made herself available to him if she had wanted to, and as a result, he never stopped longing for her. This pining for a mother who, though physically present, remained emotionally unavailable, is echoed by Gloria Vanderbilt, who experienced similar circumstances: "My mother . . . How I longed to merge into her, to disappear into her so that no longer would I be separated from her or separate from her. No longer would I exist . . . for to know the mystery of her would be to know the mystery of myself. It was all I hoped for."

3

Identifying Prime and Auxiliary Sources of Love

In the previous chapter, I pointed out that children rely on their intuitive sense of an adult's ability to provide love, and that this is the most important basis for choosing a Prime Love-Giver. *Gender, biological parenthood, and the quantity of time spent together are not nearly as important to children as how much love and devotion they believe each parent can give them.*

In some families, the difference between the Prime Love-Giver and the Auxiliary Love-Giver is very clear. Society, too, assigns predetermined duties to males and females in their social role as marriage partners, helping to differentiate the emotional roles of PLG and ALG. In the following description of Dwight D. Eisenhower's family life, not only do his parents seem to play out their social roles exactly as prescribed, but their emotional connection to the children as PLG and ALG are also very clearly demarcated.

Eisenhower's mother Ida was the greatest personal influence in the lives of her six sons. According to his biographer, it was his mother who "supervised their chores, made their meals, selected and mended their clothes, soothed their hurts, praised their accomplishments, and lightened the atmosphere in that authoritarian home." Her laughter came as quickly and as easily as her sympathy. The youngest of the Eisenhower brothers wrote in his diaries that his mother

32

had much to offer in the way of personality and joy, while his father David exercised the authority in the home.

Eisenhower's father is described by biographer Stephen Ambrose as a man who hardly ever allowed a smile to cross his face. As the unquestioned head of the household, he was tough and stern, with a quick temper that sometimes terrified his children. He was distant and aloof, and hardly ever discussed their activities, their hopes, or their dreams with them. He practiced precision in everything he did, keeping his own affairs in order and refusing to tolerate disorder of any kind from the rest of the family.

Sometimes his wife would threaten the children with reporting an instance of bad behavior to their father. The consequences of his discipline could be quite serious. Once he gave Dwight's next-oldest brother a severe beating with a leather strap, which left both boys traumatized.

In any family, you can soon guess which parent is more likely to be chosen as the Prime Love-Giver. What follows is a description of *six general traits* that we can use to help differentiate the Prime Love-Giver and the Auxiliary Love-Giver.

The Prime Love-Giver	**The Auxiliary Love-Giver**
(1) is more relaxed and easygoing	(1) functions with more tension and anxiety
(2) values human feelings above the demands of time and order	(2) has a reality-based attitude to life that places emphasis on time and order
(3) does not make stringent demands on her/himself	(3) makes stringent demands on her/himself
4) accepts the capability of the individual	(4) has high expectations of others

The Prime Love-Giver	The Auxiliary Love-Giver
(5) can be convinced to change her/his point of view; flexible	(5) is not easily swayed from her/his point of view
(6) is relatively lax about matters of discipline	6) believes in the discipline of self and others

If you look at these descriptions, you'll see that the Prime Love-Giver, like Dwight Eisenhower's mother Ida, tends to be less demanding, less controlling, and generally more relaxed with the children than the Auxiliary Love-Giver (in Eisenhower's case, his father). Disciplining children and controlling their behavior aren't high on the Prime Love-Giving parent's list of priorities, since for this parent, practical concerns always come second to human feelings. The Prime Love-Giver usually accommodates other people's ideas, feelings, and opinions, and is more easily influenced by them. This parent might be described by some people—often by the Auxiliary Love-Giver—as the more *soft-hearted* partner. Eisenhower's mother is a typical instance of this kind of caring and indulgent prime parent.

The Auxiliary Love-Giver is usually the more *tough-minded* partner. Like Eisenhower's father, the ALG tends to believe in self-discipline and in applying those standards of discipline to others. This parent believes that the demands of daily reality—which could be summed up in the phrase "It's a tough world out there"—are far more important than personal or emotional considerations. On the whole, the ALG tends to operate at a higher overall level of tension and, because this parent is more exacting, can often appear to be judgmental and hard to please.

The difference between a Prime Love-Giver and an Auxiliary Love-Giver is *not* a value judgment but merely a difference in parenting *styles*. In many ways, it simply reflects the fact that one parent feels more relaxed about life than the other. The PLG tends to be more sympathetic to the children's point of view and less inclined to judge them harshly. The ALG, on the other hand, tends to be more demanding and less willing to give in to their complaints.

As a general rule, if a parent tends to be preoccupied with adult concerns like punctuality, order, cleanliness, and discipline (topics that are rarely important to children!), the children are likely to see this parent as less loving than the parent who isn't as concerned about these issues. Likewise, any parent who is self-involved or emotionally detached from the children, as Eisenhower's father was, tends to be viewed by them as less loving.

Once the PLG and ALG have been chosen, their roles are dramatically played out in the great majority of families. Said one mother who was the Auxiliary Love-Giver: "Frankly, I'm the one who lays down the law in our house, and everybody knows it. I'm not ashamed. Whenever the kids want something they can't have, they go to their dad." On the other hand, the familiar retort "Wait till your dad gets home" reflects a Prime Love-Giving mother who, like Eisenhower's mother, finds it difficult to discipline the children herself but easy to threaten them with the possibility of their ALG father doing the job.

One thing to remember is that the division of parents I've just described is the *most common* way that the PLG/ALG arrangement takes place in a family. There are many variations on the way parents separate into their respective roles. An Auxiliary Love-Giver, for example, might be depressed and withdrawn or an obsessive workaholic, rather than a tough-minded disciplinarian. However, it doesn't matter exactly how each parent's role is manifested. The central theme of Family Theory—the division of parents based on their emotional importance to their children—remains the same. Regardless of each parent's actions or motivation, almost any parent can be identified as either a Prime or an Auxiliary provider of love.

The Prime Love-Giver

The role of a Prime Love-Giver is clearly a loving and indulgent one. Here is an example.

It is said of Lady Glamis, mother of the Queen Mother, who raised ten children, that she "loved nursing her ever-present babies." She thoroughly enjoyed reading to her little ones while they perched on her lap, taught them herself to read and write, and routinely took them on outings to visit neighbors. As soon as the children were old enough, they were included at the table during family lunches and at tea time. One of her sons reported in his diaries that by the age of about seven, all the children had an excellent mastery of the Bible stories their mother had taught them.

People generally acknowledged that Lady Glamis was comfortable and easy in her running of her family's life. She was known for her calm and happy nature and her tactful persuasiveness. She rarely felt the need to be stern with her children. Her sister once said of her: "If her older children felt that she was often less strict with the younger, experience had shown that it caused no harm to be lenient."

As we've discussed, the Prime Love-Giver in any family is the parent who is the more understanding and empathetic. She or he is gentler toward the children, gives in to their demands more often, and is generally more responsive to their need for love and attention. The children prefer to be with this parent, and are closer to him or her on both an emotional and a physical level. They're likely to discuss their most intimate problems with the PLG and are more prone to miss the PLG if a separation occurs. Children seek out their Prime Love-Giver when they want to be indulged, and they feel very competitive about getting the PLG's attention.

Although the Prime Love-Giver may not express her or his gentler feelings in an obvious way, there is always the sense that this parent is more soft-hearted and less inclined to follow through with harsh disciplinary measures than the other parent. The PLG is the one whom the children perceive to be most understanding of their demands and most willing to fight for their interests.

Both the Auxiliary Love-Giver and family outsiders may believe that the PLG gives in to the children's whims too often. It might even look to others as if the children take advantage of this parent. In fact, it's all too common for the ALG, as well as outsiders, to frequently express this opinion to the Prime Love-Giver. I will return to a discussion of this problem later in this chapter.

Variations on the Choice of Prime Love-Giver

Although it is less common, the more tough-minded parent is sometimes selected to play the role of Prime Love-Giver. A tough-minded parent might be chosen if, for instance, the soft-hearted one is emotionally alienated from the family or is inaccessible for some reason.

If the softer parent is, say, a workaholic or is chronically depressed, the children may simply be unable to form a loving relationship with this parent. The physical availability of the prime parent, which we discussed earlier, is also important in choosing a PLG. If the softer-hearted parent is rarely at home, perhaps because he or she travels a great deal, the time that the parent and child spend together will be much too limited to allow a prime relationship to form.

Finally, there are cases in which a tough-minded parent aggressively interferes in the softer parent's relationship with the children. She or he badly wants the role of PLG and, as a result, actively tries to prevent the softer-hearted parent from developing what would normally be a strong connection with the children. In such cases, the softer-hearted parent may step aside in order to avoid continual family conflict, abdicating the position of PLG to the more aggressive parent.

The Auxiliary Love-Giver

The Auxiliary Love-Giver *can* play a crucial supportive role in sustaining a family's emotional life. However, it's fair to say that this parent has a choice as to how much to become involved in the family and whether to play a positive or negative role.

The Positive Role of the Auxiliary Love-Giver
Good Auxiliary Love-Givers are vital to a family's harmony. In the best-case scenario, the positive ALG takes an active part in the family's emotional life by reinforcing the notion among all family members that there is plenty of love to go round. The positive ALG increases the overall warmth of the family atmosphere and adds immeasurably to the family's general feeling of success and happiness.

Most importantly, an ALG possesses a mysterious ability to create a sense of *belonging* among the family members. This feeling of belonging is emotionally nourishing for parents and siblings alike, and tends to create a stable atmosphere that can be crucial to preventing children from becoming alienated from the rest of the family. I discuss this feeling of belonging in more depth in Chapter 8.

The emotional backup that a good Auxiliary Love-Giver can give *to the Prime Love-Giver* is another invaluable contribution to family life. If the Auxiliary Love-Giver is supportive, the PLG can function more effectively, both as the leader of the Circle of Love and as the provider of prime love to the children. A loving ALG also allows the Prime Love-Giver to keep cool under pressure. With the ALG's support, the prime parent finds it easier to cope with the children's irrational outbursts and to remain objective in times of stress. Here is an example:

> When his marriage broke up, Mike was distraught. He was well aware that there were problems with his wife, JoAnn, but he had hoped that their active social life would compensate for any distress she might be experiencing in the home. Unfortunately, JoAnn took the three children and moved back to live with her parents in her home town. Knowing that the children were very attached to their mother, Mike didn't contest the divorce or the custody order in her favor.
>
> In his second marriage to Sue, Mike invested considerably more effort, having learned from his previous experience. He not only loved and admired Sue, but fully

appreciated the simple home life that she offered him, along with her two children, whom he eventually adopted. Even though they sometimes disagreed and at times he felt she was much too lenient with the kids, he made a point of supporting and respecting his wife. This was especially true when it came to making decisions about the children's welfare, since he recognized that she was the best judge of what was good for them.

For her part, Sue felt she was lucky to have found a man who was as generous as Mike, and who could enhance her family's feeling of security and well-being as much as he could.

Above all, the ALG's support implies that *she or he accepts and respects the PLG's vital role in the family.* This, in turn, leads to greater harmony between the partners in the marriage. Naturally, the more solid the ALG's support, the more positive the marital relationship and the greater the potential for happiness and security among all the family members. In our example above, Mike was able to play this kind of positive role as ALG in his second marriage.

Another key contribution that the Auxiliary Love-Giver can make concerns discipline. Auxiliary Love-Givers tend to have a more reality-based view of life, and they generally have more experience—and more success—than Prime Love-Givers in disciplining their children and controlling their behavior. ALG s are also slightly more emotionally removed from their children, so when it comes to deciding how to discipline a child, they can frequently be more objective and less emotional than their Prime Love-Giving partners. It's important to remember, though, that the ALG should keep a *balanced* perspective and not get carried away with disciplinary measures that are too harsh, as Dwight D. Eisenhower's father once did. Should the ALG go too far with discipline, the PLG must shield and protect the children to the best of her or his ability.

The children come to sense that their ALG is the disciplinarian. By contrast, they know that their PLG typically gives in more easily to their demands, regularly fails to follow through with threats of punishment, is less consistent in controlling their behavior, and allows them to "get away with murder" more often. Because of a generally more indulgent nature, the PLG is likely to get tangled up in situations where he or she knows that some discipline should be imposed, but feels helpless to actually do anything.

In these cases, the Prime Love-Giving parent may call for the ALG's assistance. This doesn't mean that the ALG should always be saddled with the role of "bad cop," or that the PLG should be the "good cop" all the time. If at all possible, both parents should decide on disciplinary measures together, and try to enforce them together as well.

The family in which there is a warm and competent Prime Love-Giver accompanied by a caring and supportive Auxiliary Love-Giver has the best chance of producing emotionally well-adjusted children. This is, in fact, as close to the ideal of equality as parents can hope to come in most instances. Their cooperative effort does place more emotional responsibility on one parent than on the other, but it also assumes that the second parent provides support for the Prime Love-Giver. If both parents are comfortable with this arrangement, it can allow the children to grow up healthier psychologically, and also make the whole family happier.

That's why a study of Family Theory and its subtleties is useful not only in dealing with your children but also in understanding your spouse's—or father's or mother's—points of view as well as your own. Family Theory recognizes that while the ideal family is one where the parents cooperate, we must face the fact that realistically, this rarely happens. This is because of the tendency of parents to spontaneously divide into their respective roles as ALG and PLG, and to then view the family from their own individual perspective.

The Negative Role of the Auxiliary Love-Giver

From the outside, Marie and Tony seemed to have an ideal life. Tony was a good husband by many people's standards. He worked long hours and was often tired in the evening, but he was a good provider. It was usually well past 7:00 p.m. when he got home, which meant that all the major quarrels among the three children had been settled and they were ready for bed. Tony ate his dinner, watched TV until he fell asleep, and then went to bed himself. At 6:30 a.m., he got up to do an hour of exercise, and left the house at 7:45, just when everyone else in the family was waking up for school. On weekends, he often watched sports on TV or went out to play some golf.

One Saturday night when they were out together, Marie said, "Ted is getting awfully rambunctious these days. Yesterday he hit his little brother and gave him a nose-bleed."

"Marie, you're just too soft with those kids," Tony retorted. "They'll never grow up right if you don't teach them, starting now. I'm too tired to do the disciplining when I get home. I thought that's why you stayed home all day—but I guess you can't even do that right."

"Oh, and I suppose I should let an ogre like you take over," Marie snapped. "Last time, all you did was hit him and leave him sobbing. A fine father you are. You do nothing with your kids, and then you go slapping them around like crazy!"

Fortunately, Marie did have a great deal of help and support from her mother, who joined her on most of her daily outings with the children and who would babysit for her almost any time she needed it. In later years, Marie credited her mother with keeping her marriage together, and her children psychologically stable.

While many Prime Love-Givers receive positive input from their ALG, many, like Marie, do not. An Auxiliary Love-Giver might decide to be minimally involved with the children, as Tony was, and in addition provide little support to the Prime Love-Giver in times of stress. The bitter or oppositional ALG can interfere in the PLG's valuable work by constantly contradicting or criticizing this parent's actions, thus adding to the stress that the prime parent already has to face with the children from day to day. Let's say the Auxiliary Love-Giver, like Tony, has a highly disciplinarian, black-and-white view of raising children, while the Prime Love-Giver, like Marie, is comparatively lax and sympathizes with the children's feelings. Tony's loud and angry disagreement with Marie could well undermine her authority and compromise her respect in the children's eyes. Lacking Tony's support, Marie would be forced to try to carry on dealing with the children single-handedly, while at the same time fending off Tony's criticism.

There's no doubt that an unsupported PLG is faced with an emotionally wearing situation that places a great deal of strain on this parent and, by extension, on the entire family. If these differences persist, and particularly if parents tend to argue in front of the children, all the family members will suffer. The children will be hurt, upset and unsettled by their parents' ongoing disagreement, and an emotional distance can develop between the parents that could destroy the fabric of the marriage itself.

The punishment-versus-understanding dilemma is a common area of conflict for many parents. They routinely argue about whether a good parent should be tough, demanding, and a disciplinarian, as an Auxiliary Love-Giver like Tony is inclined to believe, or lenient, easygoing, and trusting, as any Prime Love-Giver, including Marie, is likely to think.

Unfortunately, not only do parents often have quite different points of view but they are also severely critical of each other's parenting style. The ALG's and PLG's approaches are usually so different, in fact, that it's frequently difficult for parents to find a middle ground and work out a compromise. As time goes by, they often find themselves clinging more and more steadfastly to their beliefs and, as a result, being driven farther and farther apart.

In some cases, the ALG may actually be jealous of all the love, effort, and attention that the Prime Love-Giver devotes to the children. The auxiliary parent may feel resentful of holding a secondary parenting position, and actively compete with the PLG for the children's love. Or the ALG may criticize and undermine the prime parent as a way of upsetting the balance between the PLG and the children. Sometimes, without any malice intended, the ALG may merely be trying to make her or his presence felt in the family fold in order to alleviate a feeling of being excluded from it. The PLG who is aware of this feeling can respond by trying to increase the ALG's involvement with the children, or even candidly confronting the distraught ALG.

By far the healthiest role that an Auxiliary Love-Giver can play, then, is a respectful and supportive one. *The ALG's positive input is the glue that keeps the PLG and the whole family together.* The ALG should not forget that the PLG's role is extremely stressful, and that this parent's constant monitoring of the children's behavior and emotional well-being is essential. If the PLG's efforts get no support, or if the PLG has to face the ALG's continual obstruction and disagreement, this will inevitably have a damaging effect on the overall family atmosphere and will take its toll on the children's behavior.

Comparing Prime and Auxiliary Love-Giving Roles

The Permanence of the Prime Love-Giver

In Family Theory, the selection of a Prime Love-Giver is a strong and permanent decision. Once a PLG is chosen, the connection between this parent and the child becomes extremely powerful and resilient. *The choice of Prime Love-Giver is meant to last a lifetime.* It is very uncommon for any child to change her PLG once this loving connection has been established and has become part of the pattern of family interaction. Here is the case of a family that is familiar to most of us.

In the family life of Princess Diana and Prince Charles, it is quite apparent that Diana is the Prime Love-Giver for the children. She has always been the one to tuck them into bed and kiss them good night. She has been present during their crises and their successes, and has always been conscientious about protecting them and maintaining a profound emotional connection with them—this in spite of her marital crisis and efforts on the part of her husband's family to be rid of her. More disruption and antagonism in her life is created by the media and other sensationalists, who regularly spy on the family and intrude on their private lives.

The connection between a Prime Love-Giver and a child bears a note-worthy resemblance to the "bonding" that both John Bowlby and Mary Ainsworth propose in their discussions of Attachment Theory. According to this theory, bonding occurs between a mother and her child within the first few days or weeks of life and forms the basis of the child's psyche for a lifetime.

In Family Theory, the *quality* of deep and everlasting attachment between a Prime Love-Giver and a child is similar to the process that is described in Attachment Theory. However, rather than occurring exclusively between mothers and their children, this connection or "bond" can be formed with either the mother or the father as Prime Love-Giver. In fact, any competent and willing adult, such as an adoptive parent, can become a Prime Love-Giver for a child.

Family Theory also maintains that this important psychological connection occurs *at approximately six months of age*, rather than in the first few weeks. This means there is still time to establish a relationship with a Prime Love-Giver if one hasn't been formed before the child is six months old. Past the age of six months, such a relationship is profound and unchangeable. Although other good relationships will likely exist in a child's life, *there is not, and probably never will be, a relationship that can match the one with the original Prime Love-Giver in terms of its intensity, its tenacity, and its importance for the child's psychological development.*

Separation from the Prime Love-Giver
One of the most traumatic events in the life of a child is to be separated from the Prime Love-Giver for an indefinite period of time.

When Princess Diana was seven years old and her brother Charles only four, their mother, Lady Frances Spencer, lost custody of her four children, mainly because of the power and influence of her wealthy spouse, Earl Spencer. As a result of the separation from their Prime Love-Giving mother, who retained very limited access to them, Diana and Charles, the two youngest children in the family, suffered a great psychological trauma. Charles would cry for his mother every night for months, and Diana would lie in her own bed, sadly listening to him.

As a mother herself, Diana seems to have recognized her vital importance to her own children's emotional well-being. Wisely, she battled for her share of custody over Princes William and Harry. Wisely, too, she resisted the urge to escape England and its pressures by moving to another city such as New York, a move that would have distanced her from her children. Regardless of how well William and Harry might have fared with nannies and the rest of the royal family, there is little doubt that Di's decision to remain as involved as possible in her children's lives was the correct one, and that they might have suffered significantly without her, as she and her brother did when her own mother left home.

If we compare the relationship of a child to a Prime Love-Giver, such as Princess Diana, and the Auxiliary Love-Giver, such as Prince Charles, we find that strong feelings of love and mutual dependence are generally not as intense between children and their Auxiliary Love-Giver as they are between a Prime Love-Giver and the children. This is even more true when the ALG is emotionally detached from the family. Reunions with the ALG at the end of a day, say, are usually not as joyous as those with a PLG, and the activities shared by the children and their ALG are not as emotionally charged as when the PLG is on the scene.

This difference in the intensity of feelings that children express toward their PLG, as compared with their ALG, applies not just to positive emotions like sympathy and mutual caring, but also to negative ones like anger and irritation. This makes for greater pain between the children and their PLG during angry moments, but at the same time, this profound emotional connection leads to a strong urge to reconcile differences. In spite of heated arguments, basic communication with a PLG is rarely lost entirely, while in the ALG's case, less important disagreements can more easily lead to alienation.

Given the deep emotional ties between children and their Prime Love-Giver, it's easy to understand why separation from the PLG is more traumatic than separation from the ALG. If the PLG becomes unavailable for any reason, such as abandonment, divorce, or death, as Princess Diana's mother did, the Auxiliary Love-Giver can't automatically replace the lost PLG. Even an excellent Auxiliary Love-Giver cannot hope immediately to take the emotional place of a Prime Love-Giving parent, although the ALG may be the most likely candidate after such a loss.

In fact, separation from a PLG closely resembles the process of *mourning*. If children lose their PLG permanently, they need to go through a process of emotional healing similar to mourning. Only after undergoing periods of intense anxiety and perhaps denial, followed by anger, deep sadness, and finally acceptance of the loss, can a child be expected to adapt to a substitute for the prime parent. Even so, the emotional scar from losing the original PLG can be expected to last a lifetime.

For the same reason, it is hardly realistic to try to replace a lost Prime Love-Giving parent with a complete stranger, such as a foster parent, a step-parent, or an adoptive parent.

Children's Different Behavior Around a Prime and Auxiliary Love-Giver

If you look at most families, you'll find that one parent always seems to bring out rivalry or misbehavior among the children. It sometimes seems strange to us that children can behave perfectly when one parent is in charge, but as soon as the other parent comes on the scene, the picture abruptly changes: whining, nagging, and fighting erupt out of nowhere. Here is a typical example.

> Donald and Miriam are loving parents who both care deeply for their children. Miriam's work as a teacher means that most of the time she gets home earlier than her husband. For an hour or so at the end of each day, Miriam spends time with her son and daughter and helps them with their homework. The children usually play quietly together while she starts making supper.
>
> What Miriam can't understand is what happens when Donald returns from his office. "I just don't get it," she once said to a friend. "The kids and I are doing fine, having a great time, and they're getting along well. But the minute Donald sets foot in the house, all hell breaks loose! One kid starts arguing with the other and next thing I know, the little one is in tears."
>
> Donald, on the other hand, doesn't seem to think it's much of a problem. Sometimes it gets on his nerves, but most of the time he goes along with it. "They're good kids," he says, "that's all that matters. I don't mind if they jump all over me when I get home."

Children's varying behavior with their two parents is an instant clue as to whom they see as their Prime Love-Giver. While they may be on their best behavior as long as the Auxiliary Love-Giver is in charge, they will suddenly change gears and begin to act up in the presence of the prime parent, the parent with whom they feel more comfortable to let loose. Annoying and inexplicable though this sudden mood change may be, not only to the ALG but to the PLG—the person, after all, who is trying to supply as much warmth and affection to the family as he or she can—parents often experience this kind of behavior from their children. The PLG is, in a sense, held hostage by the children. The prime parent's presence provokes a kind of emotional blackmail in the children, usually revolving around rivalry or some other attention-seeking maneouver.

When Miriam, like many other Auxiliary Love-Givers, sees the chaos that inevitably takes over once her PLG husband arrives on the scene, she finds it all too easy to be critical. The ALG typically has a cut-and-dried vision of family life and has little insight into the PLG's emotional trials. The Auxiliary Love-Giver frequently feels that events should unfold in a particular way, and that any disruption of routine is to be avoided. This parent leaves only a limited amount of room for flexibility, and has little doubt about how problems with the children should be handled. When a rule is set down in the home, it is to be followed. Disputes should be settled quickly, with the parent's word as the final authority. Any talking back from a child is usually met with a swift reprimand or some other unequivocally negative response designed to discourage any further challenge to the parent's authority.

The PLG doesn't, of course, enjoy the children's misbehavior—what parent does? But as we've already discussed, the prime parent is usually incapable of imposing strong disciplinary measures to get the children under control. As a result, when the children misbehave around the PLG, the ALG's typical response is, "You brought this on yourself, so you'll have to suffer the consequences. You're too soft, and the children take advantage of you. All you have to do is be a little tougher with them [like me] and they'll get the message." To add insult to the Prime Love-Giver's injury, the same cry is often echoed by well-meaning outsiders, who tend to offer, unasked, the opinion that the Prime Love-Giving parent is far too generous and indulgent with the children.

In the meantime, it's impossible for the PLG to keep up a tough attitude. In any case, that kind of attitude isn't necessarily a workable solution to the problem of controlling children's behavior, as we shall soon see.

4

The Beginning of Favoritism

In the vast majority of families, sooner or later a second child is born. Regardless of how long the parents waited to have another child and how much effort they made to prepare the first child for this event, the emotional structure of a family is permanently changed with the arrival of a new baby. For everyone concerned, things will never be the same again. All the loving connections that have been formed must now be adjusted to include the youngest family member. The two examples that follow are typical:

> May Gruber was a savvy businesswoman who built a knitting-mill empire in New York. In her autobiography, she vividly describes her bewilderment as a young girl when she was displaced from her position of honor as the only child in the family after the birth of her little brother. When the new baby arrived home, May, already seven years old, was moved to a bedroom that had been vacated by a boarder and was separated from the rest of the house by a long corridor. She was indignant about this "reward" for being a big girl, and was left feeling lonely and isolated. Her reaction to her change in status was twofold: "I revved up my motor to fight for a first-born's rightful place," she

says, "but I also reverted to a helpless little girl; I became a chronic bed-wetter."

For psychiatrist and family theorist Rudolf Dreikurs, the memory of the birth of his sister, who was five years younger, also stands out as a traumatic and earth-shattering event that left a powerful imprint on his later childhood. His diaries tell of the resentment he felt over his sister's entry into the world. This came to be expressed mainly in the form of a severe eating problem: he refused to eat much for many months.

The birth of a new child into the family always seems to take the first one by surprise regardless of how much parents may try to prepare him. For a start, the first child's status is suddenly reduced to that of a sibling. The baby's arrival also raises the same critical question that had to be answered for the firstborn child: Who will become the new child's Prime Love-Giver and who will be his Auxiliary Love-Giver? Will the PLG and ALG positions remain the same as for the first child, or will they be reversed?

How the Second Child Chooses a Prime Love-Giver

You might logically assume that the second child would become strongly attached to the Auxiliary Love-Giver, since this parent is not as emotionally occupied with the first child as the Prime Love-Giver is. Under this arrangement, each parent would be paired off with one of the children, forming two Circles of Love in the household and giving each parent equal emotional responsibility in the household. From the baby's point of view, if she were to choose the ALG, she would face less direct competition from the older child over the love of this parent.

The other possibility is that the second child selects the existing Prime Love-Giver to be hers as well. You might assume that this, too, could work well, since the two children could *both be loved equally* by the

PLG. In this case, the children—and any future siblings, for that matter—could have parallel relationships and participate equally in an expanded Circle of Love with the PLG.

You'll remember that when the first child selected her Prime Love-Giver, she relied mainly on judging the *amount of love* that one parent could provide as compared with the other. The second child, in choosing a Prime Love-Giver, relies on this and more. The PLG's obvious ability to nurture and care for the older child, and to lead the Circle of Love, makes this parent very attractive to the new baby. In addition, the younger sibling can't help but notice the deep satisfaction—indeed the glory—that the older child derives from a wonderful, intimate relationship with the PLG.

While adults are not necessarily aware of this kind of special emotional connection, their children, as we've said, are acutely sensitive to it. It's clear that, from a child's point of view, membership in the Circle of Love is extremely attractive. While adults are all too ready to ignore or deny the Circle of Love's existence and its psychological importance, its magnetism is irresistible to children. *For children, the Circle of Love is a very special place of comfort, and being part of it is enormously important for them, emotionally and psychologically.*

For these reasons—the attractiveness both of the PLG and of the Circle of Love—a second sibling will always fall headlong into the original pattern established by the first child. *Predictably, and almost without exception, the second child will try to link himself with the same Prime Love-Giver as the first one.*

In practice, then, the prospect of two siblings peacefully forming two Circles of Love, or happily forming two parallel relationships with the Prime Love-Giver, is remote. On the contrary, both siblings usually end up trying to connect with the *same* Prime Love-Giver, and as a result, they end up as rivals. The second child finds the primary source of adult love, but quickly realizes that the first child is dependent on the same PLG. These children become adversaries or competitors, rather than allies.

As soon as one child sees another who is dependent on the same PLG as in the stories of May Gruber and Rudolf Dreikurs, the child's instincts go into overdrive. Even though the adults may be quite willing to expand the Circle of Love and add more children to it, children themselves view their closely aged siblings as arch-rivals. Their instinct to survive leads them immediately to gear themselves up to fight, in the hope either of driving the sibling out of the Circle of Love entirely or, at the very least, of pushing their rival into a less important position.

The Relationship Between the First Two Siblings

Looking at two new siblings, what will be the nature of their relationship? Can they ever be friends? Here is an example of the relationship between two well-known sisters:

> Roseanne Barr, the popular television celebrity, prefaces her autobiography with an impassioned dedication to her younger sister, Geraldine. Her words are so charged with emotion—"Where do you end, where do I begin?"—that the reader is left wondering whether Roseanne isn't being sarcastic and actually intends to deliver a powerful, in-your-face declaration of her success, which is typical of her style. This seems particularly likely in light of the fact that Roseanne makes very little mention of her sister in her book. Roseanne left home when she was sixteen, and wasn't on speaking terms with her sister for eight years after that.
>
> After they made up, the two sisters worked together to advance Roseanne's career, making little progress for a number of years. When Roseanne finally managed to get the attention of an important agent for her work as a stand-up comedian, she walked out of the auditorium alone, leaving a bewildered Geraldine behind. Instead of collecting her sister from the audience herself to share her good news, she asked the valet to bring her out.
>
> We also know that Roseanne has poor relations with her

family and has accused her father of child abuse, which provoked Geraldine to publicly come to his defense.

Given that siblings are predisposed to view each other as competitors
for the love and attention of the Prime Love-Giver, you might reasonably expect intense rivalry to erupt over the highly valued attentions of
the PLG.

This is exactly what happens to the first two siblings in a family who,
like Roseanne and her younger sister, are born and raised next to each
other. It is the essence of what we, as adults, know and recognize as sibling rivalry. As soon as a second child is born and her social instincts
come into play, this child tries to upstage the older one and monopo-
lize the Prime Love-Giver's entire attention. Since the younger child
often succeeds in this mission, she presents a real threat to the first
child. Sibling rivalry emerges automatically out of this threat.

The only condition necessary for sibling rivalry is that the children
be proximate siblings—that is, they are born next to each other in the
family. In other words, *sibling rivalry comes from the tendency of proximate
siblings to perceive each other as emotionally threatening*, and to harbor the
secret goal of somehow expelling one another from the Circle of Love.
Sibling rivalry is the way this competitive instinct is expressed.

By its very nature—by virtue of the rivalry over the Prime Love-
Giver's attention—the relationship between the first and second siblings
is filled with friction and conflict. Moreover, as a force that is natural
and instinctive, *sibling rivalry is inevitable*. It appears in every family as
soon as a second child is born. The children initiate the rivalry, which
is driven by raw instinct and is not combined with any significant powers of reasoning. Because it is instinctual, *there is no way that sibling
rivalry can be prevented by the adults who are in charge*. Siblings begin the
cycle of rivalry right from their first encounter, and never let it go.
Parents can only try their best to cope with it and keep it to a minimum.
You can think of parents—your own parents or yourself as a parent—
as innocent bystanders, unsuspecting observers of these antics.

Through their own ideas of fairness, parents may try to avoid rivalry among their children and deal with it as best they can. Generally, however, they are blind to the *depth* of their children's animosity, which persists despite all their efforts. Even though the Prime Love-Giver always expands the Circle of Love to include every new child, the children themselves continue to be poised, thanks to sheer survival instinct, to try their very best to force each other out.

How vital is this struggle to a child's psychological development? Can we ignore it and raise our children without giving any importance to the emotional impact of siblings on each other? In the past we have persisted in doing just that—discounting sibling relationships as a part of everyone's emotional and psychological growth. Parents, theorists, and mental-health practitioners have never before acknowledged the extent to which a child is preoccupied with attaining more of his parents' love, particularly the love of the Prime Love-Giver, than a rival sibling. Traditionally, psychology has placed greater emphasis on the mother-child and father-child relationships.

Family and Favoritism Theory, however, proposes that *because sibling relationships pave the way for Favoritism, they can override the psychological importance of a child's relationship with her parents.*

How Favoritism Begins

The first two siblings' struggle to outdo each other is extremely intense. Because of this, only one child effectively wins the battle for the Prime Love-Giver's attention and love, ending up with the coveted positive relationship with the Prime Love-Giver. Family Theory terms this child *Favored*, while the child who loses the struggle, and forms a weaker bond with the Prime Love-Giver, becomes the *Disfavored* child. The story of Simone de Beauvoir is a poignant illustration of the Favored-child/Disfavored-child division.

> In Deirdre Bair's biography of French writer and intellectual Simone de Beauvoir, Bair comes to the unequivocal conclusion that Simone's younger sister, Hélène, was their

mother's favorite. Simone herself, in her personal diaries, is quoted as saying that their mother was much nicer to Hélène, who possessed the quieter, gentler disposition.

Sensing this loss in her position and status within the family, Simone turned to her father, who had always been supportive of her because of her intelligence. According to Bair, this was "when the trouble really started" for Simone, since her father eventually betrayed her by joining the mother in favoring Hélène, who grew from a beautiful child into a graceful woman.

By comparison, Simone saw herself as ugly and graceless. She had none of the social ease and friendliness that seemed to come naturally to her sister. By the time she was eight years old, she had become insubordinate and emotionally alienated from both her parents. From then on, she sought refuge in her intellectualism, and everything else became secondary.

It is very important to remember that as soon as a new baby is introduced, *both* siblings, the younger and the older, have an equal chance of becoming Favored or Disfavored. If a stronger emotional connection develops between the Prime Love-Giver and the first child, then the younger sibling becomes the Disfavored one, having lost the struggle to win the PLG's affections. If, on the other hand, the younger child wins the greater part of the PLG's love, then she will become the Favored child and the older sibling will be Disfavored, as Simone eventually was.

Whether the siblings begin the cycle of Favoritism through their intense social instincts toward rivalry, or whether parents hold the key role in bringing this process to its conclusion by deciding who is Favored and who Disfavored, is a circular question, rather like the chicken-egg dilemma. One thing is certain: both parents and rival siblings are involved and, like the choice of PLG and ALG, it is an extremely subtle process that includes all family members. We see it clearly in the case of Simone de Beauvoir, whose parents were very caring and involved in all aspects of her welfare. However, try as she might through her intellectual strengths to secure their exclusive love for herself, in the end she was disappointed, and fell into Disfavor. Further examples and explanations of Favor and Disfavor are offered throughout this book and will slowly lead the reader to a deeper understanding of this phenomenon.

There's a widely held belief, promoted by Birth Order Theory, that the firstborn child is automatically the favorite. Family Theory and Favoritism, however, holds that *it is equally likely that a firstborn or a second-born sibling will emerge as Favored or Disfavored.* To prove this, there are numerous examples of firstborn children, such as Rudolf Dreikurs, May Gruber, Simone de Beauvoir, Roseanne Barr, and many others, who were upstaged by their younger siblings and remained Disfavored.

There is an equally widespread assumption—based on a popularized version of Freud's theories—that a mother automatically favors her son, while a father favors his daughter. Again, there are many examples of well-known people whose lives disprove this point of view, and certainly Family Theory rejects this notion as far too narrow.

Regardless of which sibling becomes Favored or Disfavored, the Circle of Love remains intact. Thanks to the good intentions of most parents, the Circle of Love is always widened to include any new siblings. However, for most of their lives, the children carry on a bitter underground battle for their prime parent's affection. Eventually, as you will see, *all the children of a family, regardless of their number, will be assigned either Favored or Disfavored status.*

As soon as a second child is born, a new comparative dimension is created between siblings. Each child suddenly has another child with whom to compare himself. The parents, too, have another child with whom to compare their firstborn. Favoritism, in which some personality characteristics seem preferable to others, emerges from this comparison. From now on, the children and their parents will have to contend both with the issue of comparison and, by logical extension, with Favoritism.

As time goes by, a child's position as either Favored or Disfavored becomes a fixed part of the way the family interacts, and is increasingly difficult to change. Just as a Prime Love-Giver is selected for a lifetime, a family's choice of Favored and Disfavored children tends to be deep and everlasting.

The permanence of these positions means that the characteristics associated with Favor and Disfavor become profoundly etched into each child's personality. These traits are carried through into adulthood, where much of a person's personality and behavior is determined by her status as a Favored or Disfavored child in her family of origin. This point is discussed at length in Chapters 8 to 11, but briefly, the person who was *Favored* as a child is typically relaxed, easygoing, and self-confident, while someone who was Disfavored is frequently angry, depressed, and anxious. As you will see, these fundamental characteristics are very stubborn and are difficult to change later in life, although parents can make a difference if they intervene in their children's development at an early stage. Also as adults, people can develop a better understanding of why they have become the person they are.

Age, Sex, and Other Differences Between Siblings

Most people assume that the larger the age gap between two children, the less rivalry there will be between them. But as the following example of Bill and Roger Clinton clearly demonstrates, age is of little, if any, consequence.

U.S. president Bill Clinton's half brother, Roger, was born when Bill was nearly ten years old. Though their mother, Virginia Kelley, seems to have been devoted to both her sons and tried her best to raise them well despite many hardships, there is no doubt that Bill always seemed to have the more solid claim on their mother's affections. When his stepfather, Roger Clinton—who was the first father Bill ever knew, and whose last name he later adopted—would get drunk and abusive, Bill would stand up to him and defend his mother.

As little Roger grew up, Virginia's problems with him

increased. He decided to quit school early, became addicted to drugs and learned to steal to support his habit. He was eventually sent to prison for dealing in drugs while Bill was in the middle of campaigning to be governor of Arkansas. Virginia blamed herself for Roger's behavior. In her autobiography, she says she pampered Roger too much and didn't force him to grow up, but there was probably little she could have done once his pattern of negative behavior had taken hold.

Just as with age, sex is of little relevance when it comes to rivalry. You might believe that there is less reason for a boy and girl to compete with each other than there is for two children of the same sex, but again, this simply isn't correct. Age and sex differences have practically no effect on the outcome of sibling rivalry, since rivalry is preordained by the inborn competitive instincts of the children themselves. As in the story of May Gruber who, at the age of seven, "revved up her engine" at the sight of her baby brother, as soon as a child sees another child who is dependent on the same PLG, without realizing it, his competitive instincts are automatically aroused.

Unlike adults, *children see no difference between themselves and their siblings, and have no concept of their differing needs as children of the same parents.* They are blinded by their vital need for affection. This overwhelming need means that they feel they must push aside anybody who tries to compete for the one source of love that is the most important thing in their life. It makes no difference who the competitors are: an older child will envy the attention devoted to a younger one, or vice versa; a boy will envy a girl, or vice versa; a handicapped child will envy a well one, or vice versa; and so on.

Age, sex, and other differences between children have the greatest effect on parents. From an adult point of view, if two children of the same sex are born close together, they will have more or less the same needs and interests at the same time. This makes it difficult for their parents to treat them differently. In fact, it's often tempting to lump them together and deal with them in exactly the same way.

It's easier to separate two children in their parents' minds if they are of a different sex or are far apart in age. Children who differ in age and sex are inherently farther apart in terms of their needs, abilities, attributes, and activities. As far as the parents are concerned, one child may be going to school while the other is at home. One may love to play baseball while the other is too young even to pick up a bat and wield it successfully. However, the age and sex of children have no effect whatsoever in diminishing the intensity of *the children's* emotional struggle to displace each other, since this struggle is purely instinctive.

Besides age and sex, adults also tend to classify children by their intellectual or physical capabilities. A child, however, draws no such fine distinctions. A well child may become jealous of the attention given to a mentally or physically handicapped sibling, or the handicapped child may envy the well one. In fact, it's interesting to note that, even among handicapped children, it's easy to see the dynamics of Favoritism at work. Consider the following example:

> A mother (whom most people would consider a saint) was featured on a television documentary because she had decided to keep her two retarded sons at home, rather than placing them in public institutions. The older son posed no great problem to her, as he could occupy himself during the day, follow his routines, and even hold down a menial job when he could find one. For the most part, he was gentle and reasonably easy to handle.
>
> Her younger son, a teenager like his brother, was a different story. He fought his mother every step of the way. Normal routines, such as shaving every morning, regularly turned into a horror show where the boy would lapse into fits of rage, scream, and bang his head. Once he got to school in the morning, though, he was cheerful, participated willingly in most activities, and was quite happy to spend a

good part of every day there.

Despite the fact that both boys were to some degree intellectually deficient, the difference in their behavior at home was obvious. Even as retarded siblings, these boys seemed to be playing out the normal, secret conflict between siblings for Favoritism in their household. The dramatic change in the younger brother's behavior when he reached his school seemed to reflect his feeling of Disfavor at home. He was angry at his mother for assigning him Disfavored status, but had no reason to be angry at his teachers. His older brother's gentleness, which stood in sharp contrast to his own behavior, seems to confirm his feeling of being Disfavored.

As far as children are concerned, then, their age, sex, or physical and intellectual status have virtually no bearing on their struggle to supersede their rival sibling and claim a greater share of affection for themselves.

When Is Favoritism Finally Decided?

If age has no bearing on whether a child will be Favored or Disfavored, you might legitimately ask whether there is a time when the question of Favoritism is actually settled. For example, in a case such as that of Bill and Roger Clinton, when was Favor and Disfavor decided? How old was Bill when it was finally confirmed that his brother would be the Disfavored one—eleven? twelve?

Because Favoritism is such a subtle process, we tend not to see it happening. We only presume it happened in hindsight, when we look back and see its effects on our children's personalities. To try to pinpoint a precise time when Favor and Disfavor are decided, or a time when Favoritism stops being an issue between the children, is therefore probably futile.

Just as our feelings toward our mother and father last a lifetime and remain to color and distinguish our lives forever, feelings associated with sibling rivalry begin at birth and never stop influencing children's personalities. It is safe to say, then, that the issue of Favoritism between two proximate siblings is well under way *by the time the younger sibling is one year old.* Shortly thereafter, *our* impression of Favor and Disfavor toward children probably begins to solidify. Given our present state of knowledge, then, all we can do is try to pick up the clues to this puzzle, and work within the boundaries that our children's personalities offer us at any particular time.

How Third and Fourth Children Fit into the Sibling Struggle

How do later-born siblings fit into the competitive struggle for Favoritism that is already going on between the first two children in a family?

Following the pattern described for the first two children, siblings who come after the first and second children usually choose the same Prime Love-Giver. As also discussed earlier, every child appears to be born with the ability to identify her competitors for the PLG's attention. These competitors are not all the other siblings but *only the closest ones*—those children who are born directly before, or directly after, the child and are closest to her in age. The reason for this seems to be that young children instinctively compete only with those siblings who best match their own level of ability. Children who are one sibling apart—the first and third child, for example, or the second and fourth—may also be potential competitors to some degree, but siblings farther removed than this—the first and fourth child, for instance—pose no threat to each other.

Just as in two-child families, where the parents favor one child and the other becomes Disfavored, patterns for Favoritism in three- and four-child families fall into a predictable range of possibilities. Now, however, siblings begin to form small groups called *clusters. Clusters are sets of two or three closely aged siblings who compete exclusively with one another.* All clusters are included in an expanded Circle of Love, with the Prime Love-Giver at the helm. There will *always* be rivalry within every cluster of two or three siblings, and the rivalry will be confined inside that cluster.

The Three-Sibling Family

The entry of a third child into the family does *not* upset the balance of roles, either between parents, in terms of their established positions as Prime Love-Giver and Auxiliary Love-Giver, or between the first two siblings, in terms of their status as either Favored or Disfavored. Like the others, the third child can become either Favored or Disfavored. As a new addition to the family, the youngest child may be integrated in a variety of ways. Imagine three coins with an F on one side and a D on the other. If you flip these coins, each of which represents one sibling, there are eight possible results. In no particular order, they are:

	Sibling 1	**Sibling 2**	**Sibling 3**
1.	F	F	F
2.	F	F	D
3.	F	D	F
4.	F	D	D
5.	D	F	F
6.	D	F	D
7.	D	D	F
8.	D	D	D

(F=Favored; D=Disfavored)

The above list shows all the possible combinations of Favored/Disfavored status in a three-child family. It's easy to see why, even with the help of a theory, *you can't predict the actual rivalries that develop among siblings.* Because there are so many possibilities, you have to look at the behavior of the members of your family in detail before you can figure out what combination applies to your particular situation.

Keeping this in mind, it's worth taking a look at all the possibilities one by one. The first—F F F—in which all three siblings are Favored, is, according to Family Theory and Favoritism, simply not realistic.

Thanks to the built-in competition between children for the Prime Love-Giver's attention, *there will always be rivalry between the first two siblings*, and because of this conflict, one of the first two siblings will inevitably "lose" the battle and become Disfavored.

For similar reasons, the second situation—F F D, in which the first two children are both Favored and the third one is Disfavored—is not very likely either. It would be virtually impossible for the first two children to resist competeing with each other and both become Favored. It's possible that this situation might occur under rare circumstances, perhaps if there were a very large age gap between the first two siblings, and maybe a sex difference as well. Under these circumstances, the second sibling might choose the third as his competitor, rather than the first one. But for the most part, you won't see this arrangement in families.

The last possibility—D D D, in which all the children are Disfavored—is also unlikely. Unfortunately, however, it can sometimes happen in circumstances where the family has suffered extreme emotional deprivation and there has been a complete absence of prime love for the children. All three children might become Disfavored if, say, both parents were alcoholics or abusive, and were therefore emotionally unavailable or detached from the children, or where the children were cared for in an institutional setting or reared in foster homes where they could never form lasting relationships. Under such dire circumstances—where there is no PLG and no viable substitute to whom the children can become attached—you would most likely see personality disturbances in all the children. Occasionally, they might band together, like Hansel and Gretel, and try to supply each other with the missing adult love. Thankfully, though, the conditions for this are relatively rare, since children who emerge from this type of situation do not come out unscathed.

Common Patterns in Three-Sibling Families

We are left with five patterns that can realistically occur in a three-child family. Within each pattern, there are specific areas where rivalry is most likely to occur. These areas are outlined below:

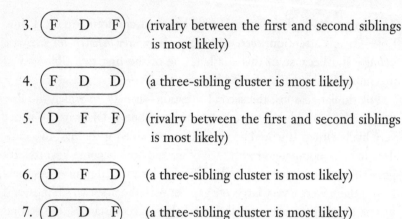

3. (F   D   F)   (rivalry between the first and second siblings is most likely)

4. (F   D   D)   (a three-sibling cluster is most likely)

5. (D   F   F)   (rivalry between the first and second siblings is most likely)

6. (D   F   D)   (a three-sibling cluster is most likely)

7. (D   D   F)   (a three-sibling cluster is most likely)

(F=Favored; D=Disfavored)

F D F

This pattern represents a family in which the first sibling is Favored, the middle child is Disfavored, and the youngest is Favored. Here are two examples:

> In a family of three children—Mike, Steve, and Jenny—Steve was always the troublemaker. He was intensely competitive with his older brother, and eventually followed his footsteps in training to be a doctor. Steve mostly left Mike alone but concentrated his anger and frustration on his younger sister Jenny, whom he picked on mercilessly. Their bickering was so incessant that their mother complained that, even when the children were in university but still living at home, she could get no peace. Jenny was lucky. Supported by her mother, she managed to survive her childhood relatively unscathed by her middle brother's anger, and went on to become a nurse herself.
>
> Melanie, the youngest in her family, was not so lucky. She had an older brother and a frustrated middle sister who was five years her senior. Failing in her attempts to compete

with the older brother, the middle sister persistently turned her anger against little Melanie, subjecting her daily to verbal insults and mild physical abuse. Soon, Melanie's marks at school fell, and eventually she dropped out altogether. She had no self-esteem and became severely depressed. Melanie is now in her thirties, regularly sees a psychiatrist, and is constantly on and off antidepressants.

In this arrangement, the conflict between the first two siblings will have begun long before the youngest one was born. Yet because the last child is Favored, there is a strong possibility that the second child, full of resentment, will mercilessly torment the youngest. However, things are not always exactly what they seem. A parent wishing to stop the endless fighting between the middle and youngest child shouldn't assume that this is where the problem lies. In fact, using our knowledge of Family Theory and Favoritism, we can surmise that the real rivalry is occurring between *the first and second children*. The parent should pay attention to this relationship, rather than being distracted by all conflict created by the younger two. This situation will be discussed at length in the final chapter.

F D D

In this situation, the oldest child is Favored, while the next two children are Disfavored. Here is an example:

> Lorne and Brenda already had two children, a girl and a boy, when their third child, Robert, was born. Robert was a difficult baby—he cried frequently and never slept for longer than two hours. Until he was ten years old he was frequently woken up by nightmares. His parents did the best they could with him, but life was difficult, and in addition, finances were strained. Lorne had a job as a hospital nurse, which meant he often had to work the night shift, while Brenda stayed at home with the three little ones. The

children were close to their mother, but she had a special place in her heart for Shirley, her firstborn child and only daughter, who was the best-behaved, the easiest to care for, and the most help to her parents.

When the children fought, the conflict usually involved little Robert and his brother. Sometimes, the two boys would gang up on their older sister, which made Brenda so furious that, although she hated doing it, she would tell Lorne when he got home, and he would give them both a good spanking. Brenda hoped things would get better when she could get out and earn some money, and the family could move to a larger house.

When the children were at school full time, Brenda took a job as a librarian and the family saved enough money to buy a house where each child could have a room. The conflict between Robert and his older brother seemed to cool a little, but it was only temporary. Pretty soon they were at it again, fighting furiously over seemingly trivial matters. Shirley was clearly the odd one out, and she openly remarked how nice it would have been to have had a sister instead of her two dumb brothers.

In their quest for the PLG's love, the Disfavored second and third children may either take out their dissatisfaction on each other, as Robert and his older brother did, or band together against the first child. Like Shirley, the first child's winning combination of Favored status and the fact that she is probably mentally and/or physically more powerful, means the effort to outdo her will inevitably be an uphill battle. However, as we know, rivalry is not an emotion guided by reason. Even though the youngest child may be at a great disadvantage, he will try to compete with the oldest one for the simple reason that he instinctively knows she is getting more love from the Prime Love-Giver.

D F F

DFF represents the case in which the firstborn child is Disfavored, while the second and the youngest are both Favored. Here is an example:

> A mother was desperate for answers to her two older daughters' constant fighting. She had scanned every book in the library in her effort to solve the problem, but to no avail. One day she sat me down on a park bench and spilled out her concerns. "I can't get a moment's peace," she said. "I can't work and I can't think—the screaming goes on from the minute they come home from school to the time they go to bed. I've tried getting them to play in the basement, but the sound of their fighting still reaches me. It's driving me crazy. Is this normal? I try to keep them apart, but somehow they always find each other and before I know it, they're at each other's throats again. The worst is when they both get in the back seat of the car, and the car is rocking up and down while they attack each other. I'm at my wit's end."
>
> After listening to her barrage of complaints, I explained that one of the girls must be feeling Disfavored. Since it was the older child who seemed to be initiating most of the attacks, we decided it must be her. My advice was to equalize the attention she gave to each of them, and to try to make the older girl feel as important as her rival, the middle one.
>
> About three weeks later, we spoke again. By now things were much calmer at home. In fact, she put her hand to the back of her ear and said, "I'm waiting for a fight to start, but it just isn't happening like before!"

The likely place for conflict in this situation is between the first and second siblings. Because the oldest girl feels Disfavored, she is attacking the middle one out of frustration. The third child is Favored and therefore happy, so it's unlikely that he or she will join an established conflict between the two older siblings. In this type of family, you might also expect to see the oldest child directing a significant amount of anger at the younger two, since they receive most of the love in the family.

D F D

In this situation, where only the middle child is Favored, we might expect this sibling to be the constant object of envy and competition from the other two, as in the following example:

> When Linda gave birth to her third boy, she was a little disappointed. She had desperately wanted a daughter, but now the family was complete. She quickly resumed her work as a physician, leaving the three boys to the care of their trusted nanny.
>
> When the baby was about three years old and the other two were six and eight, Linda noticed a definite pattern in their behavior. If either the youngest or the oldest were alone with the middle one, things seemed to go smoothly. But as soon as the three were together, the oldest and youngest would gang up on Brad, her middle one. "I don't understand it," she said to me. "He's the sweetest, gentlest of them. He loves his little brother, and he's so good to him. But that little one is such a brat. As soon as his big brother comes around, they find an excuse to beat up on poor Brad."

In the DFD situation, the siblings on either side of the middle one will try, in their own ways, to compete with this child. They may do it either separately, or together, as Brad's brothers did.

D D F

In this family, the first two children are both Disfavored, while only the youngest is Favored. Such a situation implies that love was in short supply at the beginning of the family's life. Here is an example:

> By all accounts, Roslyn was a cruel mother. She treated her three sons with equal animosity, hardly listening to them

before dealing out harsh physical blows. She rarely took them to hospital for the bruises she caused, knowing the possible consequences. When she was in a particularly bad mood, she would summon their father, who came home late at night, and he would take out his belt. If one of them got punished, they all got it.

Through it all, Jimmy, the youngest, managed to harbor some sympathy for his dad. He was, after all, a hard-working man who, because of his relatively weak personality, was easily manipulated by his hostile wife and suffered himself from her tirades and bitterness.

As time passed, the two older boys moved out and life became somewhat calmer. Jimmy would wait for his dad to come home at the end of the day, and they would regularly spend time together. When the father retired, he had even more time for Jimmy.

This did not sit well with the two older siblings, however. They resented the fact that Jimmy was able to get some of the love that had been denied them. Pretty soon, they stopped visiting home and, most painful of all to their youngest brother, refused to have any more contact with him.

If the first and second children are Disfavored, it means that, for whatever reason, no connection could have formed between them and a Prime Love-Giver. But when the third child arrives, he manages to reap enough love to form a positive relationship with one parent, and thus assumes a Favored status. In this situation, the two older siblings often experience a considerable amount of anger and jealousy toward the youngest one, as in the case of Jimmy and his brothers, since the first two children never received even the small amount of love that later became available to the Favored child alone.

Other Considerations in Three-Sibling Families
In two of the situations above—F D F and F D D—the middle child is

Disfavored. If this child starts showing signs of poor behavior, her parents will often assume that she's suffering from what Birth Order theorists call Middle Child Syndrome. According to this explanation, many middle children demonstrate problem behavior simply because they are squeezed between two other children and get too little attention.

From a Favoritism point of view, most problems that middle children experience stem from their primary rivalry with their older sibling. The arrival of a third sibling adds further stress, but it isn't the source of the difficulty. In fact, there are many middle children who demonstrate no problems at all and are wonderfully well adjusted. Birth Order Theory is unable to explain these exceptions, but with a Favoritism perspective, it's easy to explain why some middle children are perfectly happy. These are situations in which *the middle child is Favored:* D F D and D F F.

To add to the confusion that surrounds the middle child, F D F and D F D represent situations in which *the middle child is a different type from the other two*, making the middle sibling the odd one out. Children, being highly sensitive to Favoritism, sometimes see their similarities as a reason to pool their resources. Thus, two children of the same type, whether Favored or Disfavored, may band together against the one who is different. This could happen to the middle child, and create what might at first appear to be a variation of Middle Child Syndrome. But it could also happen to *any* child who is different from the other two. In our story above, for instance, Shirley's two Disfavored younger brothers teamed up against her because she was the only Favored child.

This kind of banding together—two children against one—is extremely common in triple-sibling families. Unless there are three children who are all Favored or Disfavored—which, as I have said, is extremely rare—the distribution of Favor and Disfavor is such that there must always be two of one type and one of the other in three-child clusters. This makes it highly likely that the two *similar* children will gang up on the single *different* child.

Another characteristic of three-child families is that *when two out of the three children are Favored, the rivalry will be more confined*. In other words, in situations F D F and D F F, most of the rivalry will probably take place between the first two siblings. Because the third child is Favored, he won't usually join in an active rivalry with the other two. This generally means that there is less disturbance in the household. By contrast, in situations F D D, D F D, and D D F, only one child out of three is Favored, increasing the chances of disruptive conflict. In addition, the lone Favored child is very likely to be targeted by the two Disfavored ones and blamed as the source of their discontent, as in the example of little Jimmy.

The Four-Sibling Family

My friend consulted me because she was having trouble with her seven-year-old son, John, who was acting up at home and doing very poorly in school. His father, a normally gentle and loving person, had taken to spanking him in order to control his persistent bad behavior. At the time, John had an older sister, Rebecca, and a baby sister, on whom the whole family doted.

Eventually, John was sent to see a school psychologist, who gave him a drawing test. On it he drew a house with locked doors and windows, and a family in which everyone looked angry. As a result of this test, the whole family went into therapy. Since John had a habit of talking very little, the mother proudly reported to me that her bright daughter, Rebecca, two years older than John, had taken over the session and explained all the family problems to the therapist. Meanwhile, John's behavior—the original cause of these visits—had not changed at all.

I explained to my friend that John must be feeling jealous of Rebecca because she could attract everyone's attention, including her parents', with her charming personality. I suggested that she try to better balance her attention toward her two children if she wanted to see John's behavior improve. The advice worked beautifully, and John changed dramatically.

Three years later, my friend had another son, Geoffrey. I saw the family infrequently until the youngest boy was six years old. I noticed then that he tended to look glum most of the time and stuck close by his mother. On another occasion, a mutual friend asked, "How come little Geoffrey is always hovering around you and nagging you? Why doesn't he go off and play like the rest of the kids?"

Another year passed, and my friend could stand it no longer. When we met again, she complained that her younger son, like his older brother John, was becoming difficult to handle. "Do you remember what I told you when you were having problems with John?" I asked. "Your baby is in the same position now. He envies all the attention his sweet, next-oldest sister gets. If you make him feel as important as she is, he'll certainly change." And he did. He now wears a smile from ear to ear, and is quite an independent child.

As soon as a fourth child is born, it is almost certain that the third one will become locked into a rivalry with the youngest member of the family. The third sibling's powerful inclination to choose the new child as a rival virtually eliminates the possibility that a three-sibling cluster will continue to exist among the three oldest ones.

Because of children's strong competitive instincts, *it is very rare for any child to be left out of the cycle of rivalry entirely*. For this reason, it is almost impossible for a separate, two-child cluster to form in the middle of a four-sibling bunch, excluding the oldest and the youngest ones. And only under some very limited circumstances—perhaps if there is a very large age gap between one child and the other three—would three out of the four siblings form a group, excluding one of the children at either end. Finally, as with two-sibling families, it is almost impossible that there be pairs of children who are both Favored or both Disfavored, so F F and D D combinations are eliminated.

Bearing the above restrictions in mind, imagine flipping four coins, each with an F and a D on them. Only four combinations are possible:

1. F D   F D
2. F D   D F
3. D F   D F
4. D F   F D

As in the example of my friend above who has four children, because of the predictability of these patterns, it is possible for parents to better foresee problems with their children and be prepared to address them.

Diagnosing Your Family's Dynamics

To make an accurate diagnosis of your family, or anyone else's for that matter, according to Family Theory and Favoritism, you need to follow three steps:

- **(1)** Identify the status of the parents: *Who is the Prime Love-Giver and who is the Auxiliary Love-Giver?*
- **(2)** Divide the children into their competing sibling clusters: *With which sibling does each child regularly compete in an emotionally charged way?*
- **(3)** Identify the allocation of Favoritism: *Within the clusters, who are the Favored and Disfavored siblings?*

How do you determine Favoritism? You could start by asking the members of your family what they think. However, given all children's natural tendency to complain about how they get less love than their siblings, as well as most parents' reluctance to admit they favor one child over another, you might not get too far with this line of questioning.

A more discreet approach would be to take a close look at the children's personalities. Which siblings appear to be self-confident, relaxed, and relatively content with their position in the family? These children are almost certainly Favored. In contrast, which children often express various forms of anger, depression, and anxiety? They are more than likely Disfavored.

Venturing one step further in your study of family dynamics, you can also identify certain *social subgroups* in every family. An obvious example is the special alliance between a Favored child and the Prime Love-Giver. The Auxiliary Love-Giver may also be involved in certain alliances. For example, the PLG, the ALG and a Favored child may form a close bond, to the exclusion of other children, or the ALG and a Disfavored child may find comfort with each other. In another example, discussed earlier, children who hold a similar status, whether Favored or Disfavored, are likely to band together. Thus, in a three-sibling family, the two Favored children may form an alliance against the Disfavored one, or two Disfavored children may present a united front against the envied Favored ones. In fact, it's common for various alliances to emerge and fade during the growth and development of any family.

Families with More Than Four Siblings

The famous Kennedy family included nine siblings. Their example can be used to show how, even without an in-depth personality analysis of each child in a family, it is possible, from a distance, to decipher a pattern of Favor and Disfavor among the children. At the same time, some conclusions can be drawn about the most likely patterns of clustering and competition, giving us an idea about how the children might have really felt toward each other. In the Kennedy family, it is noteworthy that Joseph Sr., the father of the clan, rather than their mother, Rose, seems to have been their Prime Love-Giver. Here is a discription of each of the Kennedy children taken from a historical biography entitled *The Kennedys: An American Drama* (Collier and Horowitz, 1984).

NAME	BORN	FAVORED or DISFAVORED	PERSONAL CHARACTERISTICS
First Cluster			
Joseph Jr.	1915	Favored	Had a dominant position in the family as the eldest son; godfather to Teddy; confident, prematurely worldly; the strongest and bravest; better at everything than Jack, and continually outgunned him; died in 1944.
John	1917	Disfavored	Had to resort to cunning and speed to outdo his brother; there were fearful fights between them, and Jack always lost; an academic and discipline problem; died 1963.
Second Cluster			
Rosemary	1918	Disfavored	Retarded; institutionalized in her early twenties.
Kathleen	1920	Favored	Nicknamed "Kick"; known as the "first daughter"; lively, vivacious, natural, lacking of affectation; died 1948.
Eunice	1921	Disfavored	Competitive, aggressive; plain, serious; a "pill"; religious.
Third Cluster			
Patricia	1924	Favored	Vivacious, star-struck; her love for her father was greater than for her husband, Peter Lawford.

NAME	BORN	FAVORED or DISFAVORED	PERSONAL CHARACTERISTICS
Robert	1925	Disfavored	Awkward, painfully shy, always wanting to please; his father recognized him as "especially needy"; later became brooding, passionate, intense; died 1968.

Fourth Cluster

NAME	BORN	FAVORED or DISFAVORED	PERSONAL CHARACTERISTICS
Jean	1928	Disfavored	Her objectives were unclear; little is said about her, except that she worked for an organization that was dedicated to the fight against Communism and corruption.
Edward	1932	Favored	The baby of the family, nicknamed Teddy; his father would light up when he saw him. (Ted's personality shows a strong depressive trait, as if his father was no longer emotionally available to him later in life, probably due to the deaths of Joe and Kathleen.)

This brief analysis of the nine Kennedy siblings gives us a picture of the pattern of Favor and Disfavor in a multi-sibling family. Although it may not be entirely accurate, it illustrates how our insights into people's lives can be greatly enhanced with the use of the Family Theory and Favoritism model. From it we get a better feel for the realities that were experienced by the Kennedy family members during their lives together.

5

Whom Do Adults Favor?

Children are not the only ones who work to bring about Favoritism in a family. Strange as it may sound, adults have the same secret agenda, although each group goes about pursuing its goals in vastly different ways. Children, as we know, try their hardest to win the exclusive love of their primary adult caregivers. Through their behavior, proximate siblings in particular manage to lure adults down the path that will eventually lead their parents into the trap of Favor and Disfavor.

But adults are certainly willing prey to these maneuvers. They have always allowed themselves to be pawns in their children's underground warfare over their love. In fact, rather than counteract the children's feud, they usually jump in and make it worse. By harboring their own list of expectations and personal preferences for their children, they add considerable momentum to the sibling struggle and contribute their own idiosyncratic twists to the final brew of Favor and Disfavor.

Just as children select a Prime Love-Giver by comparing their parents in terms of how much love they can provide, adults privately judge and select children for Favored or Disfavored status according to their own personal tastes.

Surprisingly, I've found that there is a high degree of consensus about the qualities that adults find desirable in children. Perhaps one reason for this is that most of the decisions that contribute to Favoritism are dictated by *society* at large. Other factors reflect common views held by *adults* as a group, while still others reflect *individual* preferences.

What follows is a list of common traits that influence adults in Favoring and Disfavoring children. While the list is by no means complete, it does provide an outline of the characteristics that adults generally find pleasing or unpleasant in their offspring.

How a Child's *Disposition* Can Determine Favoritism

Thomas Merton, a writer, poet, and monk who dedicated himself to finding a deeper meaning to life, writes in his diaries of his brother, Jean-Paul, who was two years younger. Jean-Paul impressed everyone with his "constant and unruffled happiness," while Thomas, a bright and willful child, was more difficult to handle.

Thomas recalls that in the evenings, when his brother was put to bed in his tiny crib, rather than protest and fight as he himself had always done when it was time to go to sleep, Jean-Paul would sing a simple tune. Thomas tenderly recalls this nice little tune that seemed very much suited to the time of the day and to the season of the year. The rest of the family would sit silently downstairs and be lulled and comforted by the baby's singing at the end of each day.

For obvious reasons, we are all drawn to a sweet-tempered child. Parents naturally enjoy a child who doesn't make too many demands on their time, sleeps long hours from an early age, eats well and willingly, and is satisfied to play alone for extended periods of time. Such behavior—what we often call a lack of "fussiness"—naturally makes life easier for the parents.

As the baby grows older, other characteristics come up for consideration. Most of us are delighted with a baby who looks happy and smiles often. We are even more pleased with a child who greets strangers openly and warmly and who doesn't protest when left in the care of unfamiliar babysitters. On the other hand, most parents' resentment mounts when their child bursts into tears and clings desperately to them at the sight of a stranger, or at the possibility of being separated from his parents.

However, if you think about it, preferring a child who isn't afraid of strangers is clearly unreasonable. For one thing, it runs contrary to our knowledge about child development. Research has shown that it is entirely normal for a baby between the ages of about six months and a year to cry at the sight of a stranger. In addition, in a few years we will totally contradict this idea when, for the sake of the child's safety, we teach her that she should not automatically trust strangers.

As a child grows up, his nature continues to be an important factor in whether he is Favored or Disfavored. As we all know, adults are attracted to an approachable, good-humored, well-behaved child who willingly does his chores and joins in activities. On the other hand, adults frequently become irritated when a child behaves in ways we consider inappropriate—through angry outbursts, crying, whining, or constantly demanding attention. The same is true if a child behaves in a seriously aggressive way, hitting or fighting with other children or even adults.

Over time, a child's behavior can become a significant factor in whether an adult treats him with Favor or Disfavor. It's important to remember, however, that the attitude of the average adult is rooted in *self-interest*. Adults are drawn to a child who respects *their* authority and is attentive to *their* instructions, both of which help the adult maintain a peaceful, organized environment. Often, a child who is unwilling to fit the mold that an adult has constructed is branded as uncooperative. Since cooperation and agreement form an important part of the *love* that can develop between two people, the child who doesn't want to cooperate becomes, by definition, distinctly less lovable than the one who is agreeable and compliant.

How A Child's *Gender* Can Determine Favoritism

Reflecting in her autobiography on the birth of her baby brother, May Gruber writes, "For my first seven years, Pa treated me as he would have a son. Over night, I had been dethroned. Had I been born the wrong sex?"

Indira Gandhi's family was sorely disappointed when she was born, and her grandmother had no qualms about showing it: "But it should have been a boy," she is reported to have said to the doctor who delivered the child. Later, an old and dying, blind relative gave Indira a blessing reserved for boys, and was spared the knowledge that a girl had been born.

When Princess Diana was pregnant with her first child, she openly declared that if she had a girl, she would try to change the rule of priority for males in the English monarchy and would fight to give a firstborn daughter the right to become Queen before a brother.

A child's sex can sometimes influence whether she becomes Favored or Disfavored. This often depends on the caregivers' *cultural background*. Many cultures still assign males greater social importance because they carry on the family name, inherit property, and pass on religious values from one generation to the next.

In the final analysis, however, it is the *individual preference* of the prime parent that exerts the most powerful influence over Favoritism. A daughter may well be Favored, for example, even though males are preferred by the society in which she lives. And a parent of either gender may long for a child of the same sex with whom to share intimate moments and emotions.

Circumstantial factors may help determine preferences, too. If a family has one or more children of one sex, for instance, the parents will almost always hope for one of the opposite sex. These preferences may even be carried through succeeding generations. A family of sons, say, may wish for female grandchildren, or vice versa.

How a Child's *Physical Attributes* Can Determine Favoritism

The physical, or aesthetic, appeal of a child can have a powerful influence on his future Favored or Disfavored status. Whatever you might think about the fairness of the situation, visual appeal has always been an important factor in attracting one human being to another. We're often unaware of our reaction to a person's looks, but at any stage in life, from babies to old people, physical appearance is part of what triggers our initial feelings of attraction to someone, which can then pave the way toward more long-term feelings of love. Naturally, looks can just as easily set off feelings of revulsion and rejection. Here is an example:

> Paula had always thought her daughter, Denise, was extremely ugly. She was ashamed of her child's appearance, and apparently couldn't bring herself to love her. It was a sad situation. Paula had three other children, of whom she was very proud, and though she seemed to have good intentions toward her daughter, she just couldn't overcome her negative feelings on facing Denise each day. As a result, Denise became a sad little girl who was starved for affection and would do almost anything to please the people around her.
>
> In a strange twist of fate, many years later, when Paula was old and her other children were unable to look after her, she was forced to live with her unloved daughter. Denise, who had suffered the pain of discrimination for all that time for no other reason than her physical appearance, was nonetheless very good to her mother until the end of her years. If she had had a vindictive nature, she might well have refused to take her mother in, or worse yet, have taken advantage of her position of power to abuse her mother in her old age.

Outward appearance is hard to resist. Like the story of Paula and Denise, what you feel when you look at another person is immediate, spontaneous,

81

and difficult to control. Paula was a victim of her own negative feelings, which translated into dislike and Disfavor of her daughter.

Although physical appeal applies to both males and females, certainly females are more frequently judged in this way. Young girls and women are continually evaluated in terms of their aesthetic appeal, a fact that seems to hold true in most societies. There are a multitude of biographical examples that bear this out. Simone de Beauvoir could not compete in looks with her pretty younger sister, their father's "Belle Hélène." Marie Antoinette was able to "marry up" to the Dauphin of France because her famous delicate beauty was highly desirable in her day. Barbra Streisand was continually reminded that she had homely features, and Eleanor Roosevelt was deeply distressed by her own assessment of herself as "an ugly duckling."

As with gender, it is generally culture that dictates how beauty is defined and which physical features are considered attractive. Preferences tend to be based on the color of a person's eyes, skin, and hair, as well as on her or his height and weight. Many societies prefer lighter skin and hair colors, combined with blue, green, or hazel eyes. Tall is usually preferable to short, while in modern times, lean has become preferable to plump.

Besides beauty, another desirable physical trait in children is agility and a light build. Adults prefer a child who can adjust her body to fit theirs when carried, one who is quick and nimble, one who crawls and walks at an early age. The desirable child does not get in an adult's way and keeps pace with the others. When an adult holds the door, the child can get in and out quickly. In other words, an agile child is independent at an earlier age and therefore gives the adult caregiver more freedom.

By contrast, a child who is clumsy, slow, heavy, or physically awkward is more troublesome to be around. A poorly coordinated child is likely to test a parent's tolerance, since she may be more accident-prone, spilling or breaking things, or falling over and hurting herself. We are all familiar with the sight of a small child in a restaurant or a supermarket who, after tipping over the glass of milk or toppling over a pile of cereal boxes, places her parent in the irritating position of having to comfort the child and repair the damage at the same time. As the child continues to be clumsy or awkward, the parent becomes annoyed with him more often and more easily, and a cycle of angry exchanges begins. Almost without realizing it, the parent can get used to being angry with the child because of his clumsy behavior, and their relationship acquires this negative foundation.

Along with other physical qualities that can contribute to Favoritism, *resemblance* deserves to be mentioned. The parent may be particularly warm and tender to a child who looks like someone the parent likes, such as a beloved grandparent. However, resemblance becomes a problem if the child happens to look like a person the parent *dislikes*. A boy who looks like his mother's abusive ex-husband may bring back bitter memories every time she looks at him. Without realizing it, this might become a basis for her dislike of her son.

How a Child's *Age* Can Determine Favoritism

The age of a child relative to siblings can lead adults to favor one over another. Here is an example from the recollections of a well-known psychiatrist and family therapist.

> Rudolf Dreikurs was treated like a pampered little prince in his middle-class Viennese family at the turn of the century. For five years he was an only child and wallowed in the attention of nannies, aunts and uncles who catered to his every whim.
>
> Dreikurs' first vivid memory is of the traumatic day when his sister Bertha was born. On waking one morning, he remembers being called to the third floor to see her. Refusing to show any excitement, he simply dismissed the whole matter to his governess as "baloney."
>
> From that time on, Dreikurs felt he never regained his privileged position. Bertha, who was quite obviously his father's favorite, managed to totally upstage her brother by playing the part of the good little sister, while Dreikurs,

increasingly angry and frustrated, acted up and received many beatings because of her. He felt defeated and hopeless because he believed he could never live up to his father's expectations, and as a result, he became withdrawn, convinced of his own inadequacy and stupidity. In school he was inhibited and did poorly, giving his father further cause to belittle him for being insubordinate and lazy.

In any family, parents will prefer an older or a younger sibling. Some parents are partial to babies because they can cuddle them and fuss over them, while others are more interested in older children, with whom they can carry on a reasonable conversation. Some people become extremely attached to their firstborn and can't loosen these ties when another child comes along. Again, culture can have a significant influence if it dictates that the first child should have special treatment, such as receiving a blessing or holding exclusive rights to inheritance.

Noting the tendency of firstborn children to become high achievers, proponents of Birth Order Theory have argued for decades that all the siblings in a family have personalities that are determined by their birth position. According to this theory, a firstborn child has a built-in advantage over the second and is the most likely to be extremely accomplished. Second children are more easygoing and carefree, while the third child is generally the most relaxed of all.

However, this is simply not borne out by reality. Many second- and later-born children achieve great eminence, and third-born children are as likely to have problems as anyone else. Most discrediting of all to Birth Order Theory, though, is that there is no designated personality status for siblings born after the third.

In contrast to Birth Order Theory, Family Theory and Favoritism attributes a large part of a child's fate to *the parents' designation of the child as either Favored or Disfavored.* Any child, no matter what his sequential position in the family, can be Favored or Disfavored. Thus, a second child, say, can easily upstage the firstborn and claim Favored status, as Rudolf Dreikurs' sister did.

Moreover, Birth Order Theory can lead some people to believe that parenting becomes diluted with later children—in other words, parents lavish less care and attention on their later-born children. Family and Favoritism Theory, on the other hand, links all clusters of siblings equally with the parents, especially the Prime Love-Giver. A later-born child, such as the Biblical Joseph, who was his father's eleventh child, can be just as important and achieve just as much as any of his older siblings. Marie Antoinette, who was the fourteenth of fifteen children, could still be Favored and have a strong and nourishing relationship with her prime parent—in her case, her mother.

How a Child's *Intelligence* Can Determine Favoritism

American writer Margaret Halsey remembers taking a standard IQ test in school and getting exactly the same score as her sister, Mary, who was one year younger. However, Margaret skipped two grades and maintained a 99 percent grade-point average throughout her academic career, while Mary brought home only average grades. How was this possible?

The difference was probably linked to another big discrepancy in the girls' lives. Their father greatly favored Mary, the younger sister, over Margaret. If Margaret dared to come home with less than 99 percent, her father would roar at her and threaten to put her out on the street. On the other hand, he was more indulgent with Mary, whose average marks were accepted without question. If Mary needed money, she had only to ask, while all poor Margaret could expect was a lecture about the value of a dollar. Unfortunately, Margaret never did recover from her father's abrasive criticism, and could not escape the damage done to her self-esteem.

Adults often use intelligence or IQ test results, as yardsticks to compare children and assign them positions of Favor and Disfavor. Most of us prefer a child who appears to be intelligent, which means the child can carry on an interesting conversation or gets good marks in school. In Margaret Halsey's case, her father harped on her apparently inadequate performance at school as an excuse to dislike her. He used powerful techniques of threat and debasement to get her to perform at a level that probably far exceeded her tested IQ.

In fact, Margaret Halsey's and others' experience has shown us that motivation frequently affects academic achievement far more than a child's measured IQ. Parents can, of course, motivate their children in a kinder way than Margaret's father! Since adults value intelligence so highly, *children often choose intellectual competition to express their underlying sibling rivalry*. Academic competition is a very *positive* direction for sibling rivalry to take, because it commands a lot of respect in our society. And once someone sets himself high intellectual standards this trait tends to become integrated into the individual's personality and spread to other areas of endeavor, which bodes well for the child in the future.

Surprisingly, though, intelligence can work against a child too. For instance, a child may use her intelligence to behave in a cheeky way, such as asking nosy questions and insisting on knowing too much about grown-up affairs. Adults experience this as an invasion of their privacy, and most find such an intrusive child irksome and offensive. Parents may become annoyed with a child who constantly badgers them for answers to impossible questions, and in so doing challenges their self-esteem. Teasing a younger sibling with questions that are too hard or showing off about good grades or other achievements can also elicit negative responses from adults.

So, while intelligence can help win adults' favor and approval, it can also provoke angry, defensive reactions if the child uses it in an irritating way.

How a Child's *Verbal Skills* Can Determine Favoritism

Verbal-communicative skills can be important in deciding whether a child is Favored or Disfavored. We are all drawn to a child who learns to talk early and well, and often favor this child over one who is less skilled verbally. The earlier a child displays an ability to communicate in words, the greater are his chances of winning our love and attention. Here is an example:

> From the time she was a little girl, Lady Elizabeth Bowes-Lyon, the Queen Mother, always impressed the many guests who came to visit their beautiful estate. As the ninth of ten children, she had a fairy-tale upbringing that included "all that children could desire."
>
> By the time she was four, she had developed a reputation as a charming, demurely polite, and amusing little girl. To one house guest, she is reported to have said: "How do you do, Mr. R? I haven't seen you look so well in years and years." At the age of five, she was overheard inviting a guest to a separate sitting room and politely suggesting, "Shall we sit and talk?" On many occasions she would assume the role of hostess and offer, "May I take you around?" and when asked, she once listed her favorite pastime as "making friends." When a particularly difficult guest showed up at the house one day, one of her sisters suggested, "Let's ask Elizabeth. She can talk to *anyone*."

It is, of course, easier for us to relate to a child who has a good grasp of language. A child who can talk confidently to adults will almost certainly be considered more likable than one who is shy, quiet, and retiring. Likewise, a solid sense of reality goes a long way toward establishing a good relationship between a child and an adult. A child who appears to understand an adult's point of view is certain to win more favor than one who seems immature, has an offbeat sense of reality, lives in a fantasy world, or is difficult to engage in conversation. Children who are creative, speak well, and are socially adept almost always impress, please, or entertain adults with their ideas and insights. But the connection between verbal skills and Favoritism is a tricky one.

Particularly if these skills develop in later life, they might signal a child's reaction to feelings of *Disfavor*. We will discuss this in greater detail in the final chapter as an aspect of social manipulation.

How a Child's *Maturity* Can Determine Favoritism

Adults find a mature child appealing. Like the Queen Mother, who adopted a grown-up way of talking to people, such a child appears to be beyond her years in intelligence and ability to communicate. Maturity suggests that the child can behave appropriately with both adults and other children.

Maturity, in other words, implies *the ability to be like adults*. We tend to prefer a child who sees the world the way we do and who appreciates our priorities. Socially mature children are better connected with the adult world. They are polite, attentive, and well-behaved. A socially mature child is also easy to talk to and better able to understand and appreciate adult conversation. Thanks to these traits, adults can communicate successfully with the mature child and feel a sense of emotional and intellectual rapport with him.

In contrast, the adult-child relationship is more strained with an immature child. This child can be tiresome and stressful to be around, since she's likely to have poor social skills and be insensitive to adults' needs. As a result, adults may end up believing that she isn't very smart, even though such an assessment usually has little to do with the child's actual intelligence.

The Arbitrary Choices of Adults

I once chatted with a mother who was very proud of her first son. He was a learning-disabled child who had achieved a great deal despite his handicap. As we spoke about the boy, she, a teacher herself, took the opportunity to inform me that her second son, who had no handicap, had achieved very little by comparison. She mentioned that since he possessed all the normal abilities, she felt he could have put them to much better use. She summed him up as being quite lazy. Not surprisingly, this son had moved away from home as soon as he could and had little contact with his mother.

Without realizing it, this woman had cultivated a much warmer relationship with her handicapped son. She had given him so much attention throughout the two boys' childhood that they had experienced this as Favoritism, with the result that she had alienated the son with no handicap and treated him as Disfavored. In her eagerness to attend to the problems of her disabled son, she had inadvertently contributed to the underachievement of the well one.

This example—in which the mother gives most of her loving attention to her disabled child, causing resentment in the well child—is surprisingly common. It clearly shows that, in the final analysis, *parents may show Favor or Disfavor toward a child on the basis of any single trait.* Some parents may favor their handicapped child at the expense of their well one. Some might favor their daughter, while others favor their son. One set of parents may favor a child for his quiet, reserved nature, while another set will be partial to the more boisterous child. Some parents will be proud of an intelligent child, while others will find the same child annoying and overly inquisitive. A parent can even become more attached to the child who cries or whines a great deal, and be more distant with the child with the more placid, independent nature.

With Favoritism, there are no rules, and efforts at prediction are futile. You'd think, for example, that if a couple finally has a girl after a long series of boys, the girl would definitely be a Favored child. But there are no guarantees that this will be so. Whether a child is Favored or Disfavored can only be discovered by looking at the *actual circumstances* of a child's family life.

6

Confronting Favoritism

Some parents openly show Favor and Disfavor toward their children. In cases of extreme Disfavor, the discrimination is unmistakable, even to outsiders. Like Cinderella, a Disfavored child is sometimes blatantly tormented by the Prime Love-Giving parent, so that the child ends up feeling that almost nothing she says or does is acceptable. The parent's disapproval can be expressed in words alone, such as constant criticism, or through actions, such as repeated and unfair punishment. This intolerance may also at times spill over into abuse, whether emotional, such as name-calling and belittling, or physical, such as frequently hitting the child. Here is an example:

> Joan was the first daughter in a family of five children. She had dark, curly hair and small brown eyes. Feeling she was rather plain looking, her parents were overjoyed when, the following year, Joan's sister was born with pretty blue eyes, and fair hair.
>
> While the parents doted on the little sister, Joan's anger at their favoring the baby grew increasingly apparent. When Dad came home in the evening, he would take the baby sister on his knee and stroke her hair. This made Joan livid with anger. When she attacked her sister, as she frequently did, she immediately tore at her hair. Faced with these

fights, both parents would intervene aggressively to protect the younger child.

Joan was slow to develop intellectually, and had many physical problems, some of which her parents attended to, but many of which were neglected. Her mother forbade her from wearing the glasses that she badly needed to correct her vision, insisting that they made her look ugly. As a teenager, she developed a strange nasal tone to her speech, and an awkward laugh, which left her socially isolated.

At the opposite extreme to blatant Disfavor, some parents become highly indignant at the suggestion that they care for one child more than another. They consider any mention of Favoritism an accusation and an insult to their personal integrity. Many are intelligent, well-educated people who feel they could never be caught in such a foolish trap as Favoritism. These parents insist that *all* their children are Favored. If they have problems with any of their children, they will likely blame external factors, such as the education system, genes, the negative influence of peers, or some other outside circumstance.

However, most parents fall into the middle range of Favoritism. They may mildly express a preference for the personal characteristics of one child over another. Many parents also see themselves as changing their favorites at various stages in the children's development. I should emphasize once again that these are parents who have always had *absolutely no intention* of loving one child more than another. Yet, as time goes on and family dynamics unfold, the Prime Love-Giver, the Auxiliary Love-Giver or both parents find that feelings of Favoritism inadvertently creep into their lives.

If most people think about it honestly, they'll gradually come to accept that Favoritism is and has always been an indisputable fact of their family life. Most people can identify someone, whether in their family of origin, their family of procreation, or their extended family, who has been profoundly affected by Favoritism. It may take time to come to terms with this new information, since it can be a disquieting, sometimes painful process. Eventually, however, it will help you understand the relationship between yourself and your own mother, father, and siblings. In addition, given time, most parents in their turn can use Family Theory and Favoritism to help find positive ways of resolving the problems with their less favored children.

The Comparative Aspect of Favoritism

Parents, like all adults, often make mental comparisons among children. An adult might think, "Rebecca is so sweet and so mature. You can really depend on her. Her older sister Jane doesn't seem to be nearly as bright or reliable."

Some adults are careful not to say anything about their preferences in front of the children. But even though they may not actually *say* the words aloud to either Rebecca or Jane, their bias is bound to be reflected in their behavior. Other adults pass verbal judgments on children as a matter of course. They may make public comparisons about how one child is better behaved or more polite or more intelligent than another. Or they may use comparisons when they're desperate to control a child's problem behavior: "Look at Johnny. He's working so quietly and *he*'s not dropping paint on the floor!"

Children care enormously about adults' approval and sympathy. This is because they are totally dependent on the love and opinions of the adults around them, particularly their parents. When the adult approves, the child glows with pride; when the adult disapproves, the child becomes distressed.

It is important for parents and other adults to remember that comparison is never separate from the judgment that lurks behind it. Behind many of the comparisons that adults make about children there lurks underlying anger toward the child. And the child senses this. All children react to a negative comparison, whether to a sibling or a peer, in exactly the same way that adults do—with hurt. Think about it. If your boss compares your work unfavorably with the work done by one of your colleagues, you might well feel like a failure. A child is no different from you or me. A negative comparison belittles the child and makes him feel inadequate.

Don't think that just because children are young, they don't notice what's going on. Children never fail to decipher the cryptic messages of criticism that lie behind any comparisons. When an adult makes a comparison, both the child who is praised and the one who is criticized clearly see the implied judgment. Moreover, comparisons open the door for future teasing. Not only will the child who has been criticized by the comparison be hurt and upset, but the child who comes off well then feels she has permission to be critical of the other, thus compounding the injury.

As part of their never-ending attempts to win the love and praise of their parents, *children participate in their own comparative exercises.* This is borne out by the fact that they seem to pounce on anything an adult says concerning the differences between them. When adults express an opinion, regardless of how casual and innocuous it may be, children tend to read far more into the statement than is actually intended. Praise for one child, for example, can easily be viewed by children as a put-down of the other. The child thinks, "I heard you say my brother reads very well and I can tell how proud you are of him. That must mean I read badly!"

Comparison, because it adds powerful fuel to the fires of rivalry, is one of the hottest coals that adults—particularly parents—can touch. While comparison is perfectly normal, it is also one aspect of adult behavior that must be altered if you wish to change the influences of Favoritism on your family. An important step toward helping a Disfavored child is not only to stop making verbal comparisons, but to try to eradicate mental ones as well. Each rival sibling has a need to be better than the other in some way. To minimize the effects of Favoritism, parents must try to be as attentive, respectful, and responsive as they can to these deep-rooted needs.

The Advantages of Confronting Favoritism

Wendy was an eldest daughter who, until the birth of her brother, four years younger, had been a sweet, adorable child. From the time her brother was born, though, her mother remembers life with Wendy as being "uphill all the way." At various times, she had her tested for allergies, hyperactivity, attention-deficit disorder, and so on, all with negative results. As the girl turned thirteen, her parents were having so much difficulty controlling her that they sought counseling. Like many teenagers in trouble, Wendy just sat there mutely, an occasional tear rolling down her cheek.

Then her mother, now pregnant with a third child, happened to read a column about my work with Favoritism and decided to give it a try. At her new baby's christening party, she presented Wendy with an heirloom necklace that had belonged to her grandmother, and Wendy was overcome with gratitude. She behaved well that weekend, and for the first time looked like she was on the road to improvement. The mother, writing to thank me, felt she had finally succeeded in making a dent in the defensive armor that her daughter had worn for such a long time.

Both father and mother, on seeing Wendy finally behaving in a gentle, responsible way and expressing her love for her family, were moved to sadness and guilt. They stayed up all night talking about Wendy, and vowed to remind one other to give her the extra attention she seemed to need so much.

Wendy's parents are typical. When people first become aware of Favoritism, they usually have to cope with a surge of conflicting emotions. Doubt, surprise, guilt, anger, and hope all jockey for attention as parents reconsider their family life as children or the current life of their children. Many pass through a period of tremendous internal upheaval.

One positive outcome of this reckoning is that the parents finally feel free to talk about Favoritism for the first time, either in terms of feeling Favored or Disfavored as a child or in the context of their feelings about their own children. This removes a great burden from many people's shoulders. Being honest about your feelings is always much easier than pretending they don't exist.

And once parents acknowledge the existence of Favoritism, they experience another positive result: the astonishing discovery of just how simple it becomes to tackle some of the serious problems they have been enduring with their Disfavored child. In some cases, parents have gone through agony over the plight of this child, some even giving up hope of ever dealing with the problem. But as soon as the issue of Favoritism is uncovered, the air is cleared. Suddenly they have the freedom to cope constructively with their personal situation.

Another source of comfort to parents comes from the knowledge that others share their predicament. To their surprise, they discover that *Favoritism is a normal and universal phenomenon in family life, and that virtually every household contains both Favored and Disfavored children.* Knowing this, parents no longer feel isolated or inadequate.

The Pressures Against Admitting Favoritism

Society's Bias Against Favoritism

There are many almost invisible social taboos that pressure parents into avoiding the whole issue of Favoritism. While our social system unfortunately teaches adults very little about parenting, the ban against Favoritism—both experiencing it and discussing it—is something that most of us seem to absorb automatically. Because of these social constraints, many parents are afraid to admit to their personal biases about their own children, even to those they trust.

As a result, parents will rarely confess to liking one child less than another. In conversation, they may try to get around their difficulties by saying their Disfavored child is "more difficult to handle" than the others, or that the child is "more stubborn by nature." They may try to rationalize problems at home by making noncommittal statements such as, "Our middle daughter isn't as gifted as the others, so we don't have the same expectations of her." Or parents may attempt to shrug off any problems by simply declaring that they have two children who are "very, very different." The whole question of disliking one's own child is highly distasteful from a social point of view. It reflects badly on the adults, as individuals and as parents, and on the image of the ideal home life that most people try so hard to build.

Understandably, parents are intimidated by the criticism they are likely to receive if they even suggest Favoritism. Nowhere is this better illustrated than in a book entitled *Siblings Without Rivalry*, by Adele Faber and Elaine Mazlish, in which a group of parents share their concerns about their children's bitter rivalries, hoping to find some solutions. At one point, a father bluntly declares, "I'll bet each person here has a favorite. I'm the first to admit that my boys are good kids, but my daughter is the light of my life." The authors respond to this remark with shock and outrage, reflecting how uncomfortable they are with the idea of Favoritism. They decide that this man seems much too relaxed about expressing a "potentially dangerous" feeling such as Favoritism. Even though other participants, obviously encouraged by this father's honesty, offer their own personal stories about Favoritism, the session is swiftly ended and the discussion of Favoritism is never revived.

These authors are quite right in thinking that the man had touched on a minefield when he dared to mention Favoritism. Unfortunately, they were at a loss as to how to deal with it, and ended up avoiding the topic altogether. By failing to respond to this man's heartfelt declaration, they reinforced, albeit unwittingly, the oppressive social taboo over Favoritism. Despite being candid about his true feelings, this father had his knuckles squarely rapped, and everyone contributing to the discussion or reading the book was served with one clear message: *Keep your feelings of Favoritism well hidden!*

Dealing with Social Myths
1. The Heredity Myth
Social myths are responsible for a large part of the anti-Favoritism pressure. One of the most popular is that a child's behavior is determined by heredity. As I mentioned in Chapter 1, Family Theory and Favoritism holds that heredity is far too simple an explanation for many

children's actions. In fact, the heredity myth is directly contradicted by many studies involving identical twins. While identical twins share exactly the same physical features, they rarely develop the same personality. Consider this true story about two twin sisters.

Susan and Sally are identical twins. When they were small, their parents dressed them in the same clothes and swore they had treated them the same way throughout their childhood. The girls got along well and rarely got into serious arguments or fights. They seemed genuinely to like each other and spent a fair amount of time together.

Susan was always more talkative and made friends more easily, although Sally, too, had a number of close friends, many of whom played on the same school sports teams. In fact, most of Sally's social activities revolved around sports. She spent hours playing basketball and swimming at the local pool.

When she was thirteen, Susan started going to parties and developing an interest in boys; like many girls her age, she spent hours experimenting with makeup, hair, and clothes. Sally, on the other hand, didn't seem particularly affected by the onset of puberty. If anything, she behaved as if she'd rather ignore it. She continued to immerse herself in sports, and for the first time, actively cultivated an image that was quite different from her sister's, cutting her hair slightly shorter than Susan's and wearing a distinct style of loose-fitting clothing.

By the time Sally was fourteen, she began to feel that there was a definite difference between herself and her sister, and that their parents ought to know. With something of a sense of relief, she finally declared, when she was sixteen that she was a lesbian. It was a secret that the whole family already seemed to have intuitively understood. Her parents were more surprised than horrified. The girls had received what their parents believed was an identical upbringing, yet Susan was heterosexual and Sally was not. How could this happen?

If identical twins have exactly the same genes, why don't they develop exactly the same personality? How could they develop a different sexual orientation, as in the case of Susan and Sally? Whatever effect heredity may have on behavior, the influence of the environment seems to be more important. This means that, despite what you inherent through family genes, you can still be pushed into a certain personality pattern by your surroundings. Within this framework, there is plenty of room for a factor such as Favoritism to leave its indelible mark.

The clear personality differences that occur between identical twins strongly support an environmental theory of personality development. As you will see in more detail in Chapter 12, identical or fraternal twins develop their personalities in exactly the same way as regular siblings. In other words, besides some minor modifications that allow for the fact that they were born at the same time, twins also tend to split into Favored and Disfavored positions, just as if they were ordinary siblings.

An equally convincing argument against the myth of heredity comes from our own experience. Many parents, as well as many prominent theoreticians, have noticed that proximate siblings routinely have different personalities. In fact, it is a rare parent who can say that they have two children born close to each other who are very much alike. Whatever characteristics one child has, the other one seems to have exactly the opposite: if one is stubborn, the other is cooperative; if one is organized, the other is untidy; if one is an optimist, the other is a pessimist; if one is active the other is slow; if one is intellectual, the other is anti-intellectual, and so on.

This difference between proximate children seems to be more than just a coincidence. Even though they may share similarities with other siblings in the family, it is certainly strange that *most proximate siblings are routinely different.* How can this pattern be so predictable? Can it be that there is a psychological force that drives proximate siblings to develop opposite personality traits? It's difficult not to conclude that, despite heredity, *something happens in the children's environment that leads to this difference.* Heredity alone can't be held responsible, since it is entirely random. The inescapable conclusion is that it would be a grave mistake for parents to fixate on their child's heredity as the source of his personality and exclude the environment in which the child is raised.

2. The Myth of a Perfect Family Life

Another myth that we all hold dear promises bliss and personal fulfillment through marriage, parenthood, and family life. This ideal misleads parents about what to expect from their spouse and children. Whether or not they are aware of it, most adults eagerly subscribe to this fiction and are often greatly disappointed when it doesn't materialize.

The myth of a perfect family has been held out as a reality in our society for a long time, particularly through television and movies. Like the fairy-tale ending, the "happily ever after" theme has dominated the way family life is portrayed. However, society is slowly coming to a more candid view of the family. Today, TV comedies regularly poke fun at the uncomfortable issues that actually arise in the home. The uncontrollable behavior of some children, the disinterest of some parents in their children, the refusal of some parents to play their traditional roles, divorce, single parenthood, and the like have all been brought out into the open. These more realistic pictures are gradually helping to eliminate the expectation of a perfect family life and making it easier to accept that most people will, in fact, face many difficulties when they raise a family.

3. The Myth of Family Bliss Without the Disfavored Child

Along with the myth of the perfect family goes a more secret, even shameful myth: that family life would be completely blissful without the Disfavored child. Parents who subscribe to the myth of the perfect family—and there are many of them—privately imagine that if only the Disfavored child weren't there, the family's life could actually approach the ideal of perfection that they carry in their heads. More than they would ever like to admit, they wish their Disfavored child would just disappear. Believing that this child was the product of some unfortunate turn of events that was completely beyond their control, they think, "What a wonderful time we could have if only it weren't for this child. We were so unlucky to have had him!" Hidden deep within themselves, they believe the Disfavored child stands between them and the elusive happy ending. Inevitably, they also feel resentful toward this child who is supposedly ruining what could be a happy family life.

Yet the notion that life would verge on perfection without the Disfavored child, or that this child is responsible for all the disruption in the family, is just another deception. This becomes clear when parents accept that having both Favored and Disfavored children in a family is virtually inevitable. If parents want more than one child, they will almost certainly end up favoring one more than the other. In fact, if the Disfavored child were actually to disappear, what would happen is simple: *another child would automatically take his place as the Disfavored one.*

4. The Myth of Sibling Loyalty

This myth is best illustrated by the fairy tale of Hansel and Gretel. According to this fantasy, parents imagine that siblings should feel a deep, instinctive love and commitment toward one another (much like the instinctive love we imagine between mothers and their infants). Parents seem to get a lot of pleasure from the illusion that their children will always love each other dearly, that they will grow up to face a hostile world together and that they will be close friends for the rest of their lives.

With your knowledge about the sibling struggle for the position of Favored child, however, you can now see what's closer to the truth: *Siblings born in sequence are much more likely to be rivals than devoted friends. This rivalry can last a lifetime, and it can only be overcome with a great deal of effort on the part of the parents.*

In fact, the story of Hansel and Gretel presents the unusual case in which the children had a common enemy—the wicked stepmother—and were abandoned in the wild to fend for themselves. When children are deprived of their parents and are thrown together to battle unfortunate circumstances, they may well form a lifelong bond in the absence of a Prime Love-Giver. However, that kind of occurrence is rare in Western society, where children are normally raised in as much comfort as possible. Ironically, it is precisely these *secure* surroundings, where a Prime Love-Giver is present, that seem to result in the emergence of Favoritism and rivalry over the PLG's love.

Emotional Reactions to Favoritism

In addition to the social pressures imposed on parents from the *outside*, there are also emotional reactions to Favoritism that come from *inside* every individual. The experience of coming to terms with the realities of Favoritism is more emotionally draining for some parents, who will take all the issues to heart, and less so for others, who will shrug them off more easily. But most parents are confused by the sudden upsurge of feelings and need help to clarify them. Here, then, is a list of some of the emotional reactions you might expect in yourself when you begin to face the facts of Favoritism.

1. Guilt and Shame

A sense of *guilt and shame* seems to be the first and foremost reaction from parents who confront Favoritism. They are ashamed to admit their feelings of Favoritism toward their children, even to trusted friends, relatives, or each other, because they believe that preferring one child over another reflects badly on themselves and their families.

And indeed, it is a painful admission. The mere mention of Favoritism seems to reach into the hearts and souls of all responsible parents. They are beset by a sense of wrongdoing: "What have I done? How could things have gone so wrong, when I meant well?" Their shame and guilt may be so strong that initially they are overwhelmed and conclude they have done something grossly immoral. Harsh self-blame and demoralization may be the unfortunate result.

Guilt is particularly prevalent in the Prime Love-Giver, who is usually more emotionally involved with the children, whether Favored or Disfavored. To many PLGs, the thought that they are not distributing love freely and fairly among *all* the children can be shocking. The idea of Favoritism may look like an attack on the parent's sense of fairness and equality. The parent may think, "It's just not in my nature to play favorites. I love my children equally." In fact, Prime Love-Givers characteristically harbor the feeling that they are so full of love and warmth, and so eager to spread it around, that it is unthinkable that this love has not been getting through to their own child.

The guilt of most parents who recognize Favoritism extends to include a strong sense of responsibility for the life of the Disfavored child. Conscientious parents are tormented by the thought that they may have contributed to their child's suffering, and find it hard to forgive themselves. If the child has become alienated from the family or is experiencing serious difficulties in some area of life, or if the relationship between the parents and the child is seriously affected, the parents may blame themselves for this failure, as Virginia Kelley did with her son Roger Clinton. The thought of possibly having contributed to the damage of their child's life can be devastating.

If you feel that way, you should remember that you are not alone in your predicament. Up to now, nobody knew any better when raising children, but after the emotional upheaval of adjusting to Favoritism, it will help you to finally begin taking positive steps toward changing the situation.

2. Sadness

Sadness is the next most predictable reaction to the sudden recognition of Favoritism, and perhaps the most difficult to confront. The sadness comes from all the time, effort, and sense of personal identity that a parent has invested in the Disfavored child. For the Prime Love-Giver, a large part of her or his own identity may be tied in with these feelings of grief: "I am sad for my Disfavored child, and sad that, despite all the love I know I have to give, the relationship between us has still gone sour."

There may be other reasons for sorrow, too. In much the same way as the Disfavored child, parents often feel betrayed, misunderstood, and trapped by what has happened to them. Nobody seems really to appreciate how hard they have tried. They pity the poor Disfavored child who, because of their misguided efforts, missed out on so much love. They deeply regret the precious time that has gone by and is now lost forever. Inevitably, they are also plagued by memories of distressing past events, those painful times that made their life, and that of their children's, so much more difficult than it need have been.

3. Self-esteem

A parent who examines Favoritism for the first time may go through a loss of self-esteem, for in taking responsibility for the way in which the Disfavored child has been treated, the parent's own worth is put at stake: "How could I have fallen into this trap? Have I just been blind and foolish, or am I really cruel and heartless?" The feeling of failure, combined with the parent's sadness, may lead to a temporary state of depression. The remorseful parent thinks, "How could I have missed my child's messages about needing more love and attention, when he made it known to me in so many ways?"

4. Anger and Blame

When parents finally confront their feelings of Favoritism, they may find no target for their anger and thus *blame* themselves. They see their own behavior as responsible for the quagmire that has developed in their relationship with their Disfavored child. Feeling inadequate as parents, they flog themselves for having misunderstood the emotional signals, convinced they should have been more attentive to their Disfavored child's veiled calls for help. Adding to their misery, they also regret the anger and blame they directed at their poor Disfavored child. Some parents of Disfavored children were themselves Disfavored, or even abused, when they were young, and vowed never to repeat the cycle with their own children. When they discover that they have in fact been caught up in Favoritism, they make the mistake of seeing their actions as a repetition of their own painful past, and worry about their sanity.

Spouses are prime targets for anger and blame. The Prime Love-Giver may get angry at the Auxiliary Love-Giver: "If only you'd been more help to me in raising the children, this wouldn't have happened!" The ALG may also become annoyed: "This is what happens when you don't use enough discipline. If you'd been stricter all along, this child wouldn't be so hard to handle now." Or either parent may try to place the blame for Favoritism on the other spouse: "*I* don't hate my child, but I know my partner does. That's what causes the problems in our family."

The discovery of Favoritism means that some anger is inevitably directed at the Disfavored child, who is usually the object of a lot of the family's anger anyway. Initially, parents may choose to believe that everything was the Disfavored child's fault; it was *his* provocative behavior that pushed them into favoring the other children. They might feel they were forced, against their own will, to love the other child more. They might argue that they tried extremely hard to show their Disfavored child that they loved her, but she rebuffed all their efforts. They might add that they are actually spending more time with the Disfavored child than with the Favored one, which is often true because of the demanding and dissatisfied nature of many Disfavored children.

Lacking a specific target for their anger, some parents may rage at external factors beyond their control: their child's friends are a bad influence, the education system is substandard, the family lived in poor circumstances when the children were growing up, and so on. Or they may decide that professionals and society are responsible, as in: "I went out of my way to consult with doctors and therapists! Why didn't anybody tell me that my child is feeling Disfavored?"

To calm themselves, parents mustn't lose sight of the fact that our current knowledge about human emotional development is so limited that it leaves most people, including professionals, groping in the dark for answers to many behavioral problems with children. Unfortunately, having been sidetracked for so long by traditional views on child psychology, and having ignored the real issues that plague parents and children in ordinary families, little additional knowledge has accumulated in the last half century that could have been of any real help to them.

5. *Denial*

Some parents *deny* their complicity in their Disfavored child's lack of adjustment, and feel justified in shrugging off responsibility. They find little reason for shame or remorse, and resort to rationalizations about heredity, peer influence, financial pressures, and the like.

Some parents even refuse to acknowledge their Disfavored child's negative behavior. Hiding their disappointment, they grit their teeth and try to ignore the problem, hoping it will go away. Many parents who deny the fact that their child is misbehaving, however, know in their heart of hearts that something is going on. These are the parents who take a defensive and somewhat dishonest stance concerning their child: "Jeffrey didn't mean to do that. He really means well, you know. He just wasn't thinking." To exasperated teachers, they may say, "Is she a discipline problem in school? We don't have those problems at home. Why can't the school deal with it?" These responses, although they may initially sound protective and loyal, in fact cover up the problems with the Disfavored child and fail to confront the real issues of disharmony in the family.

6. *Anxiety and Isolation*

Finally, many parents worry about the future of their Disfavored child. They see the child as uncooperative and difficult at home, and foresee the same problems in his dealings with others, especially people in authority such as teachers or employers. The parent thinks, "If my child is lying, cheating, fighting, and constantly unreasonable at home, how will he manage when he's unleashed on the outside world, where life is so much tougher and people are not so forgiving?"

In the end, most well-meaning parents feel isolated in their plight. Most of all, isolation plagues single parents and Prime Love-Givers whose spouses are emotionally alienated or unsupportive. Unaware that most other parents share their ordeal to varying degrees, they decide to adopt a stiff upper lip. They swallow the serious setback in their lives that is caused by the rift in their relationship with their Disfavored child, and quietly withdraw to lick their wounds.

*   *   *

For the majority of parents who harbor these feelings to one degree or another, Family Theory and Favoritism holds out a very real prospect of hope. As long as parents and children are alive and well, even if they are no longer living together, there is always the possibility of improving a situation with a Disfavored child. Moreover, if parents are willing to cooperate in their efforts, the PLG and the ALG can support each other tremendously during the crisis of coming to terms with Favoritism, as Wendy's parents did on the night of their baby's christening. These efforts will be explained in detail in Chapter 11, where the antidote or remedy for Favoritism, is discussed.

7

The Mind of a Child

The difficulties adults encounter when they try to deal with children can be put down largely to the fact that they fail to understand the way a child's mind works. Since they can't see things from the child's point of view, they simply apply their own adult logic to his actions and expect the child to think, feel, reason, and behave in ways that they themselves consider rational.

When a child misbehaves, parents, therapists, and educators grope for clues to the child's intentions. In desperation, they end up asking the child, "Why are you behaving this way, when you know you will be punished?" Privately, they wonder, "Is there something wrong with this child? Or is she just not very bright?" Most often, they tend to conclude that the child is misbehaving out of stubbornness or spite and needs someone to "teach him a good lesson," as was the case with young Winston Churchill.

> Churchill had a terrible time in school. He failed most of his subjects and was unwilling to learn anything that didn't interest him. His teachers described him as "unpunctual, careless, forgetful, spendthrift, opinionated and deliberately troublesome." He also developed a notorious reputation as a troublemaker, particularly for speaking his mind and daring to disagree with his superiors. As a result, the headmaster

strapped him more frequently than any other boy in his upper-class boarding school.

When adults opt for discipline, they assume the child knows what will happen when he misbehaves, as well as understand why he should be punished. Some parents even believe their children are capable of evaluating their parents' hardship as caregivers. From an adult perspective, it's true, the parent has usually had to work very hard to make the child comfortable, but some parents expect their children to understand this: "You don't know what a tough time I've had raising you! Don't make it even harder for me by behaving badly!" In this case, the parent is trying to impress the child not only with her or his good intentions but also with the parent's daily stresses and strains, assuming that the child will be able to see things from the parent's perspective. Another parent might make the classical declaration: "Punishing you will hurt me far more than it will hurt you." Here, the adult seems to believe that the child grasps why the discipline is necessary and can appreciate the parent's personal pain in administering it, but chooses to behave badly just the same.

Admittedly, it is strange for parents to conclude that their child's mind works so differently from their own. It's hard to admit that children simply don't feel and think the way adults do, and that they don't behave according to standards that adults take for granted. It's perfectly normal for an adult to become exasperated with behavior that's so hard to comprehend. What, after all, is going through a child's head when he misbehaves? Without this information, parents are squeezed between their lack of understanding on the one hand and their surging anger on the other. Often, discipline and punishment appear to be their only recourse.

But a reward-and-punishment approach to human behavior doesn't hold water. Following Pavlov's behavioral techniques, we have found that we can effectively train animals by systematically rewarding good behavior and punishing bad behavior. We've been told that if we apply this technique to children, we can expect similarly positive results— that is, if we consistently reward a child for good behavior and punish her for bad behavior, we should be able to get her to behave as we wish. Yet in practice, every parent has discovered that, even when they consistently *reward* a child for positive behavior, there is no guarantee that the child will always do as he's told. Similarly, when we dutifully *punish* a child for bad behavior, the child may or may not repeat it. In both cases, it's hard to predict whether a child will conform to our demands or not. Surely the problem can have nothing to do with the child's ability to understand consequences, since we know that most animals are capable of understanding consequences after just a few simple trials.

Isn't it odd that, when we deal with the human animal, the most evolved of all living creatures, it is common for a child to disregard the threat of punishment and openly defy our authority? This seems to hold true even though the punishment may be frequent, severe, and consistent. The conclusion must be that, as far as humans are concerned, *the individual will reigns supreme*. Any effort to control a child's behavior with a reward-and-punishment technique has only a limited chance of success.

Moreover, at any moment the situation can backfire, turning into a battle of wills between the two participants. If the parents pit their own aims against those of their child, the argument can easily escalate and turn into a deadlock, in which any form of punishment is useless. The child will continue to defy his parents regardless of their concerted efforts to impose stronger and better disciplinary measures. If punishment worked so well, why would there be a need to repeat it so often, as in the case of Winston Churchill? We also know that some people manage to keep secrets, when severely punished or even tortured.

Clearly, in dealing with children, there appears to be a link missing— a link that has to do with *the child's willingness to cooperate*. Since the child must *want* to cooperate in order for discipline to be effective, the most efficient way of handling your child is to try to win his cooperation before you do anything. The best way to accomplish this is by having a better understanding of exactly what motivates a child's bad behavior.

Understanding the Mind of a Child

The mind of a child was perhaps best understood by two equally famous but quite different men, each in his own ingenious way. One was Walt Disney, who gave us access to the mysterious fantasy world of the child. Disney found that he could appeal to children on an entirely different level from adults, mainly through their vivid imaginations. His talent lay in being able to translate this discovery into successful commercial endeavors. In time, his revelation opened the gateway to new, child-centered approaches in entertainment and consumer psychology.

Another pioneering effort to understand the mind of a child was made by the French psychologist Jean Piaget. By observing his own children, Piaget discovered that human intelligence follows a distinct schedule of development. He found that small children in particular perceive and experience the world in an entirely different way from adults.

Like Disney and Piaget, the Family Theory and Favoritism perspective has unearthed another profound difference between the way children and adults function. This time, though, the difference does not concern children's imaginations or their intelligence, but their *emotions*.

While parents are primarily interested in raising their children to fit in with their social environment, *children are almost entirely preoccupied with satisfying their own emotional needs*. It's as if the two groups were playing the same game but with totally different rules. Parents concentrate on socializing their children so they will be able to function well in the outside world. The things that motivate children, on the other hand—their "rules," if you like—have to do with *social instincts, perceptions* and *priorities*. If we look at these rules, we find that children are programmed to feel and think in certain ways *before* they are born into the world. Two more "rules" that a child follows are *self-centeredness* and *the preoccupation with securing love*. If we can understand these basic principles, which govern a child's thought processes, we gain a much greater insight into what actually takes up most of children's time, attention and energy. In particular, this understanding then helps us plug into what tends to make a child anxious or worried.

Social Instincts

A child's behavior is guided by two inborn social instincts. The first, as we saw earlier, is *to root out one adult source of love and follow it.* Using this instinct, the child rates her two parents on the basis of their relative soft or tough nature and selects one parent to act as the prime source of love, or Prime Love-Giver.

A second inborn social instinct helps the child *to identify his closest competitor/s for love, usually one or two proximate siblings.* This second instinct directs the child to perceive only the sibling closest to him as a threat to his security and to concentrate on fighting to drive this sibling out of the Circle of Love. For a child, it is a perfectly obvious as well as an all-consuming effort. Note the example below, in which Helen Gahagan Douglas, an acclaimed politician and women's activist in the forties, automatically chooses her younger sister as her rival and develops a personality that is diametrically opposed to her mother and sister.

As long as Helen Douglas could remember, she wanted to become an actress, but to her father, this was the equivalent of becoming a prostitute. With older twin brothers who aspired to join in the family business, and a younger sister, Lillian, who was soft and good-natured, Helen's frequent clashes with her father quickly earned her a reputation as the black sheep of the family.

While she was growing up, Helen saw herself as head-strong and unreasonable. In her autobiography, she concludes that her rebellion was, in the end, "self-obstructive and foolish." Naturally, as far as her parents were concerned, she must have stood in sharp contrast to her sister, whom she describes as sweet and gentle, like their mother.

Helen finally attained her dream of becoming an actress/singer, but this career was short-lived. She went on to politics, first being elected to the U.S. Congress—a great achievement for a woman in the forties—and later running for the Senate against Richard Nixon, a race she was to lose in a very bitter and personal campaign. Helen Gahagan Douglas felt she had led a full life, and was pleased with her accomplishments.

By virtue of her position as the third child born before her Favored younger sister, Helen was waging a continuous internal struggle against Lillian, although this struggle was so deceptive as to be virtually invisible to the untrained eye.

Parents' frustration in dealing with a rebellious child like Helen must be enormous. Yet this scenario is routinely played out in families where the parents care a great deal about the welfare of their children, as Helen's parents did. In many cases the children are not castaways; quite the opposite, they go on to reach great heights of achievement, like Helen.

The flaw in our understanding of these situations resides in the difference between the world of the child and the world of the adult. Adults often don't appreciate the fact that, for a child, the Circle of Love offers an extremely powerful source of comfort and social status. The child is convinced that to be Favored by the Prime Love-Giver is of paramount importance. To be Disfavored, on the other hand, not only holds very little status but is felt to be the equivalent of *rejection*. Thus, every child is secretly constantly preoccupied with assessing her own social standing in the family relative to the rival siblings in her cluster, as Helen was, and with trying somehow to capture a greater share of love from the Prime Love-Giver than her rival.

Perceptions

A second area of difference between adults and children concerns their *styles of perception*. Suppose all children were born with a sense of smell as sharp as a dog's. We know that smells dictate a large part of canine behavior, from constant sniffing to tracking a scent or seeking out food. Yet for the human who doesn't have the same sensitivity to smell, the dog's behavior can seem bizarre. Going for a walk can be a nuisance, when the dog tugs one way—following his nose—while you want to go in the opposite direction. In an effort to train your pet, you might try to distract him, discipline him, or reward his good behavior with pats and treats. You do it for the simple reason that you have to get on with your day and the routine of walking the dog.

The same is true with adults and children. Children are constantly "sniffing around," responding to stimuli that elude their parents. *When one child sees another getting attention, particularly from the PLG, an underground emotional war is declared.* The child might hear her parents comment to a younger sibling, "You've done such a lovely drawing." Even though the adult simply means to praise the young one's effort, the older child, overhearing the remark, will almost always think, "That must mean that what I'm doing isn't as good."

These feelings of rivalry, which are a source of unbridled emotion in children, strongly influence their perception of the world, and by extension, their behavior. Yet they hardly seem significant at all to adults. Parents just aren't sensitive to the emotional cues that constantly concern their children. They can't figure out why their child becomes so upset at certain moments, and they usually have little patience for the inexplicable attention-seeking behavior (throwing a tantrum, whining, and the like) that may follow. Adults have no idea that sibling rivalry is something the child thinks about all the time, and that it dominates and orchestrates almost all of her thoughts, feelings, reasoning, and behavior. Lacking adequate tools to guide them, parents end up feeling at a loss or simply annoyed in the face of their child's apparently bizarre behavior. When their child misbehaves, they often resort to spur-of-the-moment efforts to control him, such as trying to enforce discipline through punishment, efforts that are almost always both inappropriate and unsuccessful. The child, in turn, feels disappointed, resentful, and misunderstood.

This state of affairs, in which the children's constant cues signifying rivalry are almost invisible to their parents, means that it is frequently difficult for children and adults to get along well together. Because their perceptions are so different, it's easy for wires to get crossed, resulting in a mutual lack of understanding. In many families, neither adults nor children can appreciate one another's feelings and thoughts or relate them to their own life experiences. And of course, if that emotional gap grows wider over the years, and the child's experiences become too separated from her parents', then conflict and emotional tension will inevitably accumulate.

This rift in perceptions between adults and children is a central aspect of Family Theory and Favoritism. The difference is sometimes as great as between a dog and its owner. Obviously, we shouldn't lose sight of the fact that there is also plenty of common ground between children and adults. However, I have focused on the *differences* here simply because they have never before been acknowledged.

Priorities

A third area of discrepancy between children and adults lies in their *life priorities*—the things each person considers essential to happiness and satisfaction, and which he seeks to attain. Priorities help determine your overall behavior, since they provide a large part of the motivation in your life.

One good example of the difference in priorities between adults and children is in the area of play. As any parent knows, children will make a beeline for toys, and proceed to concoct games full of fantasy and imagination. Play is an activity that holds enormous significance for children, and if a child is not allowed to play, she will inevitably become sad or angry. Yet once a child becomes an adult, the urge to play declines dramatically and is no longer a priority. Exactly the same activity somehow has much less appeal.

Even if an adult was deprived as a child and didn't have enough opportunities to play, having the chance to play later in life isn't likely to make up for the loss. The teaching assistant in my daughter's kindergarten class, for example, once told the children in an angry moment, "I wish I'd had those toys to play with when I was younger. You kids just don't know how lucky you are. You don't deserve what you have!" Here was a person who could play all day if she wished, yet the toys that surrounded her only made her unhappy.

Just as there are activities that are important to children but poorly understood by adults, there are also activities that are priorities for adults but mean nothing to children. Adults, for example, tend to value order, cleanliness and organization, which help adults structure their lives, and function more effectively at work and at home, and allow adults to maintain a certain level of physical and mental comfort.

However, as every parent knows, it's a rare child indeed who believes that order, organization and cleanliness are important or who is likely to try to pursue these goals each day. In one of Ann Landers' columns, for instance, readers wrote in about their children's messy rooms and their efforts to get them to clean up. One grandmother recounted that when her three grandsons were growing up, their rooms were always so disastrously untidy that you could hardly walk into them. Yet she was pleased to report that the two older boys, now in their twenties, were both in doctoral programs at universities, and the third was well on his way to a professional career as well.

Trying to teach our children these values is a necessary part of child-rearing. But until such activities become important to the child, he is not likely to pursue them on his own with much enthusiasm.

Self-centeredness

Judy had tried hard to prepare her two-year-old daughter, Lily, for the arrival of a new sibling. When she first came home from hospital, little Lily was affectionate toward her baby brother, patting him on the head, shoving toys in his face, or trying to help change his diapers. Sometimes, though, she would get mean and hit him. One day, when Judy was putting an attractive new outfit on the baby, Lily suddenly sprang up and declared, "*I* need that!" She grabbed the outfit and tried to put it on herself. "Bring it back here now," her mother said. "You know that's much too small to fit you." "But I *need* it!" protested Lily. "I need it too!"

On another day, Judy heard a scream from the baby's room. When she ran to the rescue, there was Lily on the floor, sucking at the baby's bottle. "This is *my* bottle," she announced loudly while her brother cried. "Mmm, it tastes good."

A child's world is built far more on self-interest, or *self-centeredness*, than most of us imagine. Both Freud and Piaget recognized this phenomenon. Freud called it *egotism*, while Piaget referred to it as *egocentrism*. In both cases, the prefix *ego* refers to the *self*.

Freud identified egotism as basic narcissism, or interest in oneself, and associated it with common acts of self-indulgence such as looking in the mirror or giving yourself a treat. Piaget identified egocentrism as an early stage of childhood thinking in which the child sees himself at the center of every event in his life, even the movements of the sun and moon. According to Piaget, this stage ends when the child is about seven years old. He then enters a more rational and adult-like phase in which egocentric thinking subsides and logic takes its place and exercises the major control over his reasoning powers.

In Family Theory and Favoritism, the term *self-centeredness* refers to immature thinking that not only places great emphasis on the self but also includes a basic lack of consideration for the rights and feelings of others. In other words, in its most raw and primitive form, self-centeredness includes outright selfishness, sometimes to the detriment of other people's needs and feelings. It is the type of selfishness that we associate with grabbing, hoarding, or even stealing things, without any thought or consideration for others. You often see this kind of selfishness among animals exercising their territorial natures and in the way that many species establish a pecking order. This same basic instinct is at the source of children's sometimes ruthless aggression over acquiring and protecting their personal possessions.

Unlike Piaget's egocentrism, however, Family Theory and Favoritism maintains that self-centeredness depends not on how old the child is but on the child's circumstances and how she's raised. *Self-centeredness begins at birth, and has no age limit for its disappearance*. It is a form of emotional immaturity that can diminish with time, but may also linger and influence a personality for a lifetime. Whether or not self-centeredness decreases in intensity depends on the child's emotional environment. *If a child is emotionally well-nourished, she will easily abandon self-centeredness and move on to being more rational.* On the other hand, *if a child is emotionally deprived, her maturity may be significantly delayed and self-centeredness may take decades to fade, or may in fact never be eliminated.* In terms of Favoritism, a child's relative security on feeling Favored will tend to promote her emotional growth out of self-centeredness, while feelings of insecurity, which are normally associated with Disfavor, will tend to stall or delay such growth.

There are a number of ways that self-centeredness can be expressed. These may be mild or forceful, obvious or secretive. Think of a child who badly wants a candy but whose parents refuse to give her one. Expressing a *mild* form of self-centeredness, the child might ask, "May I ple-e-e-ase have a candy?" In a more *forceful* way, the child might demand, "Give me a candy! I want one now!" perhaps following this with a temper tantrum. Expressing the urge in a more controlled but still *obvious* way, the child may look for the candy in every likely spot at home or head out to the corner store. But if the child is completely unable to control his self-centered desire, he may resort to *secretive* methods of satisfying the urge—stealing a candy when nobody is looking, or stealing the money to buy the candy and possibly denying it later on. Generally, children who are more Favored will have more control over their urges and desires, and show less self-centeredness, while children who are less Favored will remain self-centered until a later age.

While the mild and obvious ways both indicate a strong urge to get the candy, the child does show some control. The child who uses the forceful and secretive methods, however, lacks adequate control over the urge and will stop at little, including temper tantrums and stealing, in order to satisfy it.

Self-centeredness is a characteristic in children and adults that most of us find unpleasant, particularly when it's expressed in extreme forms. Most adults react with embarrassment and shock when they see their children acting like this. "How could my child behave in this awful way?" they ask themselves. "How could I have brought her up so poorly?"

However, despite our attempts to deny it, this kind of primitive self-ishness exists in *all* humans. When parents socialize their children, they devote a great deal of time and energy to discouraging the children's innate selfishness and encouraging their generosity and sharing instead. Every parent can remember telling a young child over and over to *share* the toys. Every parent has explained to a young child—many times—that no, the chocolates are not just for him but for everyone. Selfishness or self-centeredness exists in all small children from the moment they're born. It is a powerful and natural drive that can exert a profound influence on their behavior.

When you look at what's important to your child and what really motivates her, it's critical that you take into account *her fundamentally selfish nature.* You must acknowledge the inescapable fact that, given the slightest chance, most children will try to claim more than their right-ful share of anything. If you accept that self-centeredness profoundly affects your child's behavior, you can react differently. Say your child pleads for candy that has already been refused. Instead of questioning the child's intelligence—"I've told you three times already! Weren't you listening?"—you can ask yourself, "How far has this child pro-gressed beyond basic self-centeredness?" You are bound to find that some older children are still very self-centered, while others grow out of it much more quickly.

Instead of condemning your selfish child's behavior, you can now link it to Favoritism. You'll discover that the reason for much of your children's behavior, as well as their varying frustration levels, can be directly traced to their positions of Favor or Disfavor. Those who feel Favored and appreciated by the adults around them are likely to appear more mature and less selfish. In their behavior they show kindness and a willingness to share. Children who feel Disfavored, on the other hand, follow the social rules less often than their Favored siblings and are therefore labeled less mature. They are more inclined to try to grab and hoard things for their own purposes.

The issue of children's social maturity is critical, since it affects both their personal characteristics and our responses to them as individuals. I will return to this issue in Chapter 9.

The Preoccupation with Securing Love

The preoccupation with procuring love from adults is another factor that dominates a child's thinking. As you saw in more detail in Chapter 5, parents definitely prefer certain traits and characteristics in children, and frequently hope to fulfill some of their most cherished *personal* dreams through their children.

Although a child can never fully appreciate an adult's hopes, she still senses, at a profound, nonverbal level, the parent's longing to fulfill these dreams through her. The child reacts to these unspoken wishes by trying to please her parents, as part of her ongoing quest to win her parents' love and attention. In fact, one of the major motivations of children's behavior is *their deep desire to fulfill the wishes and dreams of their primary caregivers, their parents.*

Support for this view comes from our understanding of what concerns children and, more importantly, what they *worry about* each day. Here is an example of a girl who is so bothered by her feelings of sibling rivalry that she takes drastic action:

> The well-known American writer Carson McCullers was born in 1917. Her mother had apparently heard a prophecy that the child, her firstborn, would be unique and eventually achieve greatness as an artist, so she treated the girl like a little goddess. When her brother, Lamar Jr., was born two years later, it is reported that Carson was so much in the forefront of her mother's affections that she had no need to feel jealous of her new sibling.
>
> By the age of four, however, Carson had begun to turn into a lonely and unhappy child, signs of her feelings of Disfavor. She showed no hostility toward her younger brother, because he seemed content to follow her leadership.

But her anger came out in full force after her baby sister was born, when Carson was five and a half years old.

After a long, miserable quarantine for scarlet fever, Carson woke up one day wailing that she hated her baby sister. When her parents weren't looking, she took the baby from her crib and placed her on the hearth beside the fire, hoping she would be "consumed." Then, in a bid to capture her mother's attention, which had shifted to the baby, Carson took her little brother to a back room of the house and proceeded to light a Roman candle for each of them. The two stood there in awe and terror, watching as the streams of brilliant color from the firecrackers ricocheted off the walls.

Children simply don't have the same preoccupations or priorities as adults, as you can clearly see in the story about Carson McCullers, whose antics stemmed directly from her jealousy of her baby sister. While adults worry about reality—such things as cleaning house, making money, or putting food on the table—a child's thoughts and worries are entirely different. The child's mind is dominated by one main preoccupation: *the competition for love.* He continually asks himself, "How much love am I getting in comparison with my rival sibling? Am I getting it all, or is my rival getting more?"

This search for love can become so intense that in some instances, when children feel they are getting very little attention from their parents, even a negative reaction is better than nothing and will be coveted. One child, for example, saw her sibling get smacked for bad behavior and was heard to say, "Hit me too. I want to be bad too!"

The Sibling Struggle

Given the child's preoccupation with securing and maintaining her parents' exclusive love, it doesn't seem far-fetched to assume that the child will struggle to get rid of any person or object who might stand in the way of this love. Naturally, one major obstacle is the proximate sibling. This is the essence of what we, as adults, have come to recognize and label as sibling rivalry or *the sibling struggle*. Here is a biographical illustration of the rivalry between two sisters:

> In her autobiography, Kitty Dukakis, wife of U.S. presidential candidate Michael Dukakis, paints a portrait of herself and her sister Jinny, fifteen months younger, as two very different personalities. Kitty describes Jinny as being content with the simple things in life, unlike herself. Jinny was neat, frugal, and dispassionate, while Kitty was messy, extravagant, and emotional. Despite the fact that Kitty was close to her father—a musician who was always warm and supportive of her—she knew that her mother favored her sister. She recalls furious fights in which they tore at each other like "mini-Amazons."
>
> Her envy would peak when her mother tactlessly said to her, "You're just pretty . . . You have the looks, but your sister has the personality." Considering her mother's lack of sensitivity to the sisters' rivalry, Kitty notes, "It's a miracle we didn't kill each other."

Much to adults' surprise, children eat and breathe competition and rivalry with their siblings. In fact, most adults would be astonished to discover that *the majority of children's actions, both inside and outside the home, are geared toward getting more love than their rival sibling.* You can probably remember this preoccupation if you think back to your own childhood and your relationship with your brothers and sisters, and you can certainly see it in cases such as those of Carson McCullers and Kitty Dukakis. Children think so much about gaining—or losing—their parents' love, particularly the prime parent's, that it is no exaggeration to say that these concerns, along with which sibling is getting more love at any given moment, absorb most of children's emotional and intellectual energies.

Adults consider sibling rivalry, especially fighting among their children, a nuisance that they hope will be over quickly. For the child, on the other hand, conflict with a sibling over the love of their Prime Love-Giver is overwhelmingly serious, and the consequences can be devastating. From a child's point of view, competition with a rival sibling is a do-or-die situation. It dominates the child's every thought and action.

As I said at the beginning of this chapter, childhood thinking is basically irrational—it isn't governed by adult laws of reason or logic. And when it comes to love, children are particularly unreasonable. They view the battle for their Prime Love-Giver's love and respect as an all-or-nothing situation, in which there is no room for compromise. It makes sense, then, since this love is so enormously important to the child and since a child is guided primarily by emotions, that any child who sees someone threatening this goal will invest a great deal of energy in the struggle to win.

The implications of this fixation on parental love are far-reaching. Because the child yearns to be the PLG's *exclusive* love object, his feeling of success or failure at securing the PLG's love is intimately connected with his sense of self-esteem. The sibling struggle, then, becomes the central pivot around which the child's emotional life revolves, and its impact on a child's personality is profound. *The outcome of the sibling struggle—whether a child is Disfavored or Favored—affects the child's entire sense of purpose in life and his connection with the outside world.* Understanding this is a vital step toward understanding the child psyche. It becomes easy to see how, given the child's way of thinking, extreme behaviors connected with his anger, depression, and anxiety at feeling Disfavored can take over.

Since a child sees life in black-and-white terms, she will also see a distinct winner and a distinct loser in the sibling struggle. If she feels she's won the PLG's love and is therefore Favored in comparison with her sibling, she will also feel *extraordinarily happy and satisfied with life, and develop a good measure of self-confidence.* If, however, she senses that she is losing this crucial battle, she will become angry, depressed, and/or anxious, and will begin a lifelong struggle to gain this prestigious position.

This central factor, then, explains a lot about who you are. Who was loved more when you were growing up? The answer to this burning question determines the degree to which you feel like *a winner* or *a loser* for the rest of your life. In addition, more often than we are aware, *this struggle can become so desperate that it becomes the leading cause of many children's emotional and behavioral problems.* Many of us judge and discipline our children with little basic understanding of their motivations, but a grasp of Family Theory and Favoritism reveals that a great proportion of children's problems stem from their feelings of Disfavor as compared with a sibling.

A person's *competitive drive* is also a direct outcome of the sibling struggle. Like selfishness, the impulse to beat out your competitors has its source in humanity's primitive roots. As we all know, many animals have a pecking order by which the more aggressive animals shoulder aside the weaker ones in the competition for food or a mate, sometimes even pushing them out of the group altogether. A domestic cat or dog may become jealous when a new pet enters the home: it may show hostility toward the intruder (anger), grow sad and withdrawn (depression), or whine and become irritable (anxiety).

Unfortunately, children's competition for love is rarely as obvious as it is with pets. It tends to be expressed more indirectly and is often disguised. On the negative side, a child's struggle for love may mean he demands attention when the parent is obviously busy, by physically or verbally attacking a sibling, or by behaving in other ways he knows will irritate his parent. Yet strangely, a child who behaves in the *opposite* way shows the same fundamental need for love and attention. The child may do whatever she can to please the adult, such as being cheerful and lovable, quiet and obedient, or attentive and loving toward the adult.

Children will sometimes, though rarely, openly express their overwhelming concern about how much they are loved compared with their rival sibling. Most often, though, they aren't even aware of the link between their behavior and their need for love. Children are born with the power to reason, but with no knowledge about *the direction their reasoning should take.* As a result, every child develops according to her own individual experiences. If a child's experience with positive behavior is good, he will, for the most part, continue it. But if she gets a significant response when she misbehaves, even if the adult is annoyed or angry, she will be inclined to keep on misbehaving in the belief that this is what gets her the love and attention she craves.

When children do express their need to feel more loved than a sibling, adults, for reasons I outlined in the previous chapter, have a strong tendency to block out this information. Most parents aren't willing to acknowledge that they treat their children differently. In addition, they are usually not aware of their children's desire to outdo each other. If a child is trying all sorts of tricks to get his parent's attention, the parent may rationalize a cool response by thinking: "I'm already giving him more time and attention than the others. If I give him even more love, he'll only become spoiled." Alternatively, the parents may try to totally deny their child's friction with her siblings: "It's just a phase. She'll get over it. It's probably best to ignore her behavior—she's only trying to get attention."

Professionals, too, are to blame for their ignorance about the competitive, love-seeking behavior of siblings. For decades, they have swept aside children's complaints when the youngsters claim that another child in the family is loved more, and they have dismissed children's calls for love as inexplicable misbehavior. They have advised parents—wrongly—to ignore attention-seeking behavior, which they have termed "acting out," and have encouraged them to use discipline instead of trying to further their understanding of how children think.

Parents, for their part, have proved to be eager allies in the adult "plot" to ignore Favoritism. They tend to resist suggestions that they feel any preferences among their children, and are all too willing to discount a child's honest complaints about not feeling loved as much as a sibling. In many a therapy session, as well as at home, children have said clearly that they feel their parents love the rival sibling more. Yet these complaints have fallen on deaf ears.

However, using your new knowledge of Family Theory and Favoritism, you can see that your child's attention-seeking misbehavior is, in fact, a vital clue to her discontent over the amount of love she believes she is receiving. "Acting out" is intended to communicate the child's worry over losing the battle with the rival sibling. In this sense, what we have come to label childhood misbehavior should more correctly be referred to as *love-seeking behavior*.

In order to understand the way a child thinks, it's essential that we begin by appreciating *every* child's desperation not only to be loved, but *to be loved more than a sibling*. The phenomenon of sibling rivalry, which up till now we've regarded as inconsequential, actually reaches to the very core of the human condition, and plays an enormous role in determining the personality traits that will eventually characterize each individual for the remainder of her life.

8

Anger and the Disfavored Personality

On a television phone-in program, a woman called to consult the guest psychiatrist regarding her five-year-old son, Darren. The family had just moved to a large city, and Darren's mother had recently given birth to a baby girl. The mother was worried because her son had told her he was hearing voices in his head instructing him to "kill the baby."

One of the first things Darren's mother did was to talk to the teacher at his new school. The teacher was reassuring, describing Darren as a quiet child who seemed to be settling well into his new class.

The psychiatrist on TV asked whether Darren was eating and sleeping well, as indeed he was. Finding nothing amiss, he advised the mother to take Darren for a psychological assessment at the local children's hospital, "just in case." The doctor may well have suspected the boy was schizophrenic—highly unusual in a bright child of five-years-old. He did not mention the issue of sibling rivalry with the baby sister, nor alert the mother to the fact that the arrival of a new sibling can cause great tension in a child. Similarly, it is unlikely that Darren's feelings of rivalry would be unearthed by any professional he might see during a psychological evaluation.

126

Such potentially vicious antagonism between siblings may sound extreme. However, if you remember that the thought came out of a *child's* mind, not an adult's, it doesn't seem nearly so strange. Darren simply wants his mother's exclusive love back, and can't understand why his sister had to come along and take it away from him. Even though he has no real understanding of what "killing" his sister really means, his anger makes him wish he could just make his sister disappear.

Most practitioners and students of sibling relations tend to ignore children's anger toward their rival siblings, emphasizing instead their potential for mutual love and devotion. However, as you'll recall from earlier in the book, between proximate siblings, *rivalry is inevitable*.

A Disfavored child, or one who feels threatened by the possibility of Disfavor, as Darren did, tends to react with three main emotions— *anger*, *sadness*, and *anxiety*. These three standard human responses to distress aren't generally found independently but tend to appear *in combination*. You'll rarely find a person who is exclusively depressed, angry, or anxious. Rather, you will probably find some signs of anger, depression, and anxiety in every Disfavored person, although in most cases, one of these reactions will predominate.

Angry reactions to Disfavor can be directed at three targets: siblings, in the form of *sibling fighting*; peers, in the form of *peer aggression*; and finally, when anger is directed at parents and other authority figures, we see it in the form of *rebellion*. This chapter deals with each of these targets for anger and gives some valuable hints to parents about how to deal with each.

Anger as Aggression Toward Siblings: Sibling Fighting

As the daughter of Christian missionaries, Ruth Bell Graham, wife of evangelist Billy Graham, was raised in China with her sister Rosa, who was two years older than she was.

When they weren't playing together, the two sisters would fight furiously. Ruth would sometimes chase Rosa with dead bugs and once, she pursued her clutching a pair of scissors. Ruth Bell Graham's biography offers the following description of the young sisters' squabbles: "Their spats were like small typhoons, with their two tiny bodies virtually disappearing into a whirling cloud of flailing feet, fists, and tangled hair." Sometimes their fights were so ferocious that they attracted an audience of family servants, who would gather around the two warring children and place bets on the outcome.

When parents of siblings who fight incessantly see a family where the children *don't* fight, they naturally think, "How come these people's children get along just fine, while ours fight all the time?" But the outwardly calm appearance of a family doesn't accurately reflect what is really happening on an emotional level. True, the absence of sibling fighting makes life more comfortable for all family members, and helps them maintain a good social image. However, *peace in the household does not mean there is no rivalry among the children.*

Because sibling rivalry is instinctual, you can assume that if you don't see it in the form of fighting, it must be happening in other ways that are less visible. Fighting is only one way of expressing rivalry; it is simply the most direct and obvious evidence of children's instincts to outdo each other. Other forms of sibling rivalry, such as *intellectual competition* or a *dominance-submission pattern* between rival siblings where one child dominates the other, are far less easily observed by outsiders. Both of these "peaceful" methods of handling feelings of rivalry are discussed in the final chapter.

Some fighting among brothers and sisters is quite normal. However, if two siblings fight intensely, and almost all the time, this means that *fighting has become the principal way for them to express their rivalry.* If fighting becomes entrenched as the main way that two siblings behave with each other, it's a stubborn pattern that is difficult to change.

In attacking the rival sibling, the child thinks: "If I could only get rid of my sister, my whole world would be perfect. Even if I can't get rid of her, I'm going to do everything in my power to defend my territory against this most unwelcome intruder." The most glaring clue to the child's anger, as well as to the urgency he feels about getting rid of his "opponent," is when he confesses his raw, primitive urge to "kill the baby," as Darren did. You'll remember that Carson McCullers expressed the same wish when she placed her baby sister by the hearth and hoped she would somehow be "consumed."

Sibling fighting demonstrates the *desperation* behind a child's efforts to win the sibling struggle. The *intensity* with which siblings fight, and the *lack of logic* that goes along with the fighting, are clues to the children's underlying emotional frenzy. When they quarrel, they're not really fighting over a toy train or a place in the front seat of the car or even a common friend. In fact, the immediate subject of the fight is often so trivial that it can't possibly be the cause of all that bitterness. As anyone knows who has siblings or who is now a parent, brothers and sisters often look as if they're ready to destroy each other. No matter how sincerely parents try to be fair when they intervene, one child will probably still be dissatisfied.

Parents often ask themselves why their children act up so relentlessly when their constant bickering makes everybody around them miserable, as well as themselves. Every time there's a fight, each child seems poised to win not only the current battle, but ultimately what seems to be an imaginary war. Vital matters must be at stake here— matters of power and supremacy.

Unfortunately, some families regularly have to contend with severe arguments among the children, and every conflict seems to escalate into a fight to the finish. The children pick *any* issue as grounds to start a quarrel, and then each participant tries to destroy their opponent's mental or physical resistance. By acting this way, they can throw an entire household into a constant state of war alert, and even the most patient of parents can become utterly exasperated. If name-calling and shouting routinely overflow into physical attacks, the situation can deteriorate even further, with significant emotional costs for both the children and their parents.

What is often underestimated is not only the *serious purpose* behind sibling arguments, but also the distress of the children themselves, and the lasting effect this struggle will have on their personalities. Many sibling rivals are left with permanent bitter memories of their family life, and carry their emotional scars right into adulthood. Sometimes, the family situation becomes so intolerable, that one child feels forced to leave home earlier than is usual, simply to get away from the chronic state of pain and tension with her rival sibling.

Adults are inevitably shocked by the bitter, angry thoughts that provoke their children's fights. Lacking an explanation of why their children feel such strong emotions, most parents end up confused, anxious, and sometimes angry themselves. How can their own children hate each other so much? Why can't they just be friends? Or if they can't manage that, why can't they just stay out of each other's way?

In fact, parents themselves are also profoundly affected by their children's emotional agitation. If the arguments become chronic, they too feel upset, frightened, and victimized. But conventional therapy offers little comfort to adults who are caught in the middle of their children's struggles. Typically, professionals dismiss the problem by declaring that sibling rivalry is natural, and accuse the parents of overreacting or being overly concerned. Therapists routinely tell parents, "Don't be too worried. The children will get over it. They *need* to express themselves in this way." Or the counselor may try to be reassuring: "They'll be just fine. You don't need to interfere—they won't kill each other. You worry too much." This last piece of advice is particularly annoying because most parents can sense the obvious—*their warring children **are** in fact poised to "kill" one another, if not physically, then emotionally.*

Another fact about family life that should be given more weight is simply this: *human strife causes a great deal of anxiety for those who are forced to watch it.* When we see other people fighting, we can be profoundly affected. Even if we're not directly involved, we can become hurt and frightened ourselves.

Fighting is particularly traumatic when it occurs between people we love, such as our parents or our children. Most people accept this when it comes to the question of children who see their parents fight. Most will admit that seeing their parents arguing was one of the most frightening experiences of their childhood, and left them feeling threatened and insecure. Parents who are constantly subjected to the sight of their children battling together also suffer. Watching your children constantly fight provokes anxiety, irritation, and depression. It adds immeasurably to adults' daily stress, makes them feel as if they've failed as parents, and shatters their hopes for a blissful family life.

Another nasty consequence of children's arguments is that the parents themselves may begin to fight. Pushed to the limit of their emotional endurance, one parent may blame the other for mishandling the situation or for failing to stop it. At the extreme end of the distress scale, some parents, who find the fighting unbearable, may use it as a final excuse to escape their family entirely. Raising children is already a tension-filled and never-ending task. Like the proverbial straw that broke the camel's back, the difficulties of having to confront endlessly squabbling children, on top of shouldering the normal pressures of being a parent, can end up alienating one parent from another, and lead to separation or divorce.

How to Deal with Sibling Fighting
1. Deal with Your Own Feelings First
It's true that you're not the person who's fighting—your children are—but in order to deal with them successfully, you first have to make sense of your own feelings and expectations. For a start, *drop all your fantasies about family bliss and harmony*. Bear in mind that, as I discussed earlier, these are simply myths that society has generated, and although they have little connection to reality, they have unfortunately become deeply ingrained in most people's minds.

In order to make some progress with your battling children, you must stop imagining that sibling rivalry can ever be completely eradicated from your family. Take comfort in the fact that *sibling fighting is entirely normal* and that even serious sibling fighting doesn't mean your family is "dysfunctional." You must also remember that no matter what it looks like from the outside, no other family is truly free from sibling competition. Since the root of this conflict lies in the children's desire for the Prime Love-Giver's exclusive love, and since this stems from children's most basic social instincts, you can never entirely prevent the rivalry. The plain fact is that there never was, and never will be, a solution to sibling rivalry or sibling fighting *except to eliminate one of the children!*

Unfortunately, rather than running its course and disappearing as children grow older, sibling strife doesn't necessarily decline as time passes. With age, rival siblings still need to outdo each other and merely become more adept at hurting each other's feelings. Fighting between siblings usually reaches its peak in middle childhood, between the ages of about seven and twelve. In most cases, it fades somewhat in the teenage years, when children develop their own interests and start to become independent. However, it could just as easily carry on into adolescence and extend into adulthood, where it is likely to become more refined. There are no guarantees that it will ever go away entirely.

It's best for both you and your spouse, then, to get accustomed to the idea that your children's fighting will probably continue for a long time to come. Particularly if sibling fighting has become a habit among your children, you should brace yourselves to cope with it as a part of normal, daily life, rather than try to deny, suppress, or oppose it. Even though the road may seem to be rough and unfair at times, you are more likely to cope with the fighting successfully if you treat it as *a chronic disease* than if you struggle to make it miraculously disappear. Once you've accomplished this change of emphasis, you can begin to gear yourself to handling the problems that really underlie the rivalry in your household.

2. Don't Rely on Your Children to Resolve Their Fights Themselves

Contrary to the advice of many professionals, *disagreements between rival siblings are often not resolved fairly when the children are left to work them out on their own.* Remember that the feelings of bitterness and rage that cause their conflict are more deep-rooted than any specific argument.

As well, children are basically self-centered and aren't capable of putting themselves in another person's place. For these reasons, children can't be trusted to resolve their own disputes fairly. Left to their own devices, most of them will be guided by their self-centeredness, so that an older or stronger child will almost always try to take advantage of a smaller or weaker one.

3. Monitor Your Children's Fights Carefully

Far from being ignored, then, *sibling fighting needs to be carefully monitored by parents.* Part of this monitoring involves becoming attuned to what's *motivating* the children. Parents should listen carefully to ongoing arguments, keep track of each child's feelings of triumph or loss, and hold the idea of Favor and Disfavor in the back of their minds. Questions to ask yourself include: Is one child always attacking the other? Is one child always reacting in self-defense? Was one child clearly provoked? What is this aggressive behavior *really* about?

In other words, by listening in carefully, you should *try to identify which child is feeling Favored and which Disfavored,* and think about what the underlying causes of these feelings might be. This is tricky terrain, and it's easy to become confused, so take your time before you jump to any conclusions. A stronger or older child, for example, who is mercilessly tormenting a younger, weaker one may be expressing a powerful need for attention because she is feeling Disfavored compared with her younger sibling. On the other hand, the same scenario could describe an older child who is taking advantage of his Favored position simply for the pleasure of overpowering the weaker one. Only the children's parents are in a position to make this kind of critical judgment.

4. Intervene in Your Children's Battles to Help Settle Disagreements

Once you identify the dynamics among your children—who is Favored and who is Disfavored—it's up to you to gently step in and help balance the odds. In most cases, some interference is better than none at all. Without deliberately upsetting either the more aggressive child or the more submissive one, parents should intervene in their children's battles at key moments and tactfully try to adjust the balance of power. If this doesn't help, *they should always be prepared to interpose with more forceful measures to balance the picture.* If Joey is pinning his sister to the ground, for instance, you could say: "Joey, get off your sister. Joey, get off *now*. All right, I'm giving you three seconds—one, two, three . . ." *Time for parental intervention!*

5. Try to Be as Objective as You Possibly Can

Parents themselves often become emotionally involved when they try to control their children's fighting. Their own anger, sadness, and humiliation rise up at the disheartening sight of these children, who should, according to all the myths, be the best of friends, instead battling away like mortal enemies.

However, it's important to try to make a special effort to keep an emotional distance. It's also important to resist the temptation to take sides, even though an argument may clearly seem to be the result of one child's misbehavior. Try to steer clear of consistently penalizing one child for all the noise and trouble in the household. *Parents should try to react as objectively as possible*, both to the issue at hand and to each of their children. If you find that you're siding with one child more than another, it would be a good idea to take a look at your own feelings. Ask yourself: "Am I really being fair and sympathetic to both of my children? Am I really considering both their points of view?" From time to time, you might even talk to the children about your own dilemma, and your honest efforts to treat them even-handedly, but don't be too surprised if this has little impact.

6. Use any Method to Cope with the Fight, as Long as it Respects the Children's Feelings

When sibling fighting is intense and ongoing, *any method that works to end it is acceptable*, as long as the children's individual feelings are respected. When the children are babies, *distraction* is often useful for ending a squabble: "Oh, there's a big truck going by!" Or, "Look! I just found this toy under your chair!" Failing this, removing one child from the situation is as good a technique as any. Parents can also try *separating* their children for periods of time during the day, perhaps with the help of extended family, friends, or babysitters.

When the children are a little older, *threats, separating the children*, or *disciplinary action* can all be useful tools. Contrary to current mental-health advice, threats of punishment *are* appropriate if they actually help bring a fight under control. Although threats should not be overused and the punishment should not be too extreme, this method is perfectly valid, *even if the parent has no intention of ever carrying the punishment out.*

There's no need to worry about carrying through with discipline, and absolutely no need to worry about being consistent in your approach to an aggressive child. Family Theory and Favoritism holds that *threats are a legitimate way of controlling children's behavior,* and no adult should feel compelled to follow through with a foolish threat simply to prove to a child that she is serious and not merely a gutless parent. Sometimes, our threats are too extreme for the circumstances: "I'm going to wash your mouth out with soap" or "I'm going to get you, just you wait." As long as the child understands the message the parent is trying to convey—the fact that the child's behavior is totally unacceptable and must stop—the parent's disapproval is often punishment enough.

As their children grow older, parents may try to encourage them to develop different interests to minimize rivalry in the same area. The older the children get, the more they will be inclined to veer off in different directions to avoid encroaching on each other's territory.

7. *Decide How Much Fighting is Enough*
Throughout your efforts to mediate in your children's disagreements, you should bear in mind that some fighting is a normal part of growing up. Conflict resolution—settling fights in a fair and calm fashion—is an essential social skill and a tool that everyone must learn. A child who doesn't fight may not learn how to defend herself or how to resolve conflicts peacefully.

But how much fighting is enough? Only the parents can judge how much fighting their family can tolerate without too much disruption. As with anything else, moderation and good judgment are the keys. Complete intolerance of fighting can be as damaging as total freedom.

8. Constantly Reassure Your Children that You Love Them

Any action that parents decide to take to handle sibling fighting should always be tempered with *reassurances of their love*. As much as possible, parents should try to listen sympathetically to all their children's points of view. This is especially important with the Disfavored child, who is angry because she feels less valued. Even if the issues seem silly to an adult, parents should respond seriously to their children's distress. In fact, treating a child's emotions as important is one way of telling her indirectly that you love her and respect her. Don't be dismayed if some of your children's anger is occasionally directed at you, for this too is a normal reaction.

9. Both Parents Should Help Control Their Children's Behavior

In the effort to control sibling fighting, *the participation of both parents is likely to increase your chances of success.* For discipline to be effective, ideally both parents should collaborate and agree about their course of action. A child is far more likely to give in—and give in with less resentment— if he sees both parents insisting on the same course of action.

The importance of the Auxiliary Love-Giver in helping to maintain control during times of crisis can't be overemphasized here. As discussed in earlier chapters, it is often difficult for the Prime Love-Giver to discipline squabbling siblings or resolve their fights. The ALG, on the other hand, usually finds this process much easier and should therefore be actively involved, except in cases where she or he has a tendency to go overboard, as Eisenhower's father once did. In these instances, the ALG's actions should be tempered by the prime parent, since as we all know, discipline that is too harsh can seriously damage a child.

Even if the ALG is not the family disciplinarian but is a more passive person, a positive role would be simply to support the PLG's decisions on how to handle the strife.

Sibling Fighting Between Adults

The late British comedian Benny Hill used to fight a great deal with his brother Leonard, who was two years older. When their cousin Chris would come to spend the night at their house, Mrs. Hill would ask him to sleep in between the two boys, in the hope that it would stop them fighting. Poor Chris only ended up getting bashed from both sides.

Tired of bitter verbal battles with his father, who was known as the Captain because of his insistence that other people obey his orders, Benny Hill left home at the tender age of fifteen. His feelings about his brother never improved. They had a thorny relationship until they reached their early thirties, and then had a complete falling out, during which they didn't speak to each other for over thirty more years. No one really knew the cause of their disagreement, and they themselves couldn't even agree on why it had happened.

Finally, in their sixties, these two grown men reached a truce at the prodding of their cousin Chris, and when Leonard died in 1990, Benny felt enough closeness to attend his brother's funeral.

Children's fights are frequently both physical and verbal, although physical aggression decreases with age. It's not normal, for instance, to see a thirty-year-old brother and his twenty-five-year-old sister hitting each other! However *verbal bickering can, and often does, continue for a lifetime.*

As a sibling grows older, his rival can still arouse the same old anger, but the ways in which that anger is expressed change over the years. One of those ways is to find more *sophisticated, verbal methods* of expressing his feelings, perhaps through insults, snide remarks, or mean-spirited jokes.

Another way is to turn their rivalry into an *unspoken conflict* in which siblings refuse to see or speak with each other for extended periods of time. Later in life, spouses and children may be dragged into the conflict as well. Thus, for apparently trivial reasons, Benny Hill and his brother

Leonard, Ann Landers and Abigail Van Buren, and Roseanne Barr and her sister Geraldine refused to see or speak with each other for years.

Growing up, moving out of the family home, and especially having children are events that help take people's minds off their childhood sibling rivalry and change their perspective. Yet siblings never, ever forget this conflict and are profoundly influenced by it for the rest of their lives. Most people, even into old age, can trot out stories about what awful things their brother or sister did to them when they were young. This is all the proof we need that *the relationship between rival siblings is potentially the most antagonistic and explosive of all human experiences*. These powerful feelings are deeply etched in the minds and hearts of all siblings, and color the rest of their lives.

Anger as Antagonism Toward Peers: Peer Aggression

Some children take the anger that results from feeling Disfavored and turn it on their peers outside the home. They find other children who are smaller, weaker or more docile, and release their aggression by bossing them around, hitting them, calling them names, or otherwise instigating conflict. In the extreme form of this behavior, the child becomes a bully and causes other children physical or emotional damage. Here is an example.

> Lynn and Rita became best friends in high school. From the beginning, they could share their emotions about feeling distanced from their families. "I hate my mother—she's always yelling at me for something," Lynn would say. "My stepmother's worse," Rita would retort, "she's a greedy old bitch. All she wants is my dad's money so she can spend it on herself. Then she goes and tells him bad things about me, so he comes after me. I hate going home."
>
> One day on the way to school, Lynn and Rita met their neighbor, Jackie. She was a quiet girl, who was being raised by her grandmother since her mother disappeared five years

before. "Need some help with your books?" Rita asked in a taunting tone. "Oops—now you do," she said as she pushed a pile of books out of Jackie's arms. "Let us help you pick them up" was her next ploy, as she rifled through Jackie's things. "Now, what have we here—a wallet? Can I borrow a few bucks? I need some money for lunch today. Thanks a lot." Rita and Lynn went off laughing, leaving Jackie behind, sad and humiliated.

Danger looms when an angry child grows up to be an angry adolescent who still can't control his behavior but, because of his size and strength, now poses even more of a threat to others. Unfortunately, there are many stories about adolescent aggression, including bullying, peer pressure, and gang behavior. Research and literature on the subject have proliferated, but we still understand very little about the problem of peer aggression or how to handle it.

Faced with an aggressive child, adults are baffled. They often end up asking her, "Why are you behaving like this?" The child frequently comes back with the unhelpful response: "I don't know." Even more distressing is the child who declares that she is tormenting other children "just for fun." The adult has no idea what to think. Does the child really think it "fun" to see other people getting hurt? Does she really have no idea what prompts these actions?

Gently coaxed, an aggressive child may talk about feeling hurt and betrayed by friends or Disfavored by family members. Unfortunately, adults are often unsympathetic. Responding mainly to the child's provocative behavior, they will tell the child that other people won't like her *unless she learns to behave properly toward them first*. However, by taking this stance, they only succeed in reinforcing the child's image of herself as the one who's always to blame for the trouble. In effect, the child is being told that she is "bad" in comparison with others, thus adding to her feeling of rejection. As a result, she ends up feeling more victimized and unjustly accused.

Adults frequently add to the child's pain by contradicting his deep-rooted knowledge that he is Disfavored. If the child confesses to feeling betrayed by his family, adults often insist, "That can't be true. I'm sure your family loves you and they're trying to do their best for you. You're lucky to have them, you know. Some children have no family at all!" In taking this approach, they challenge the child's belief that he holds an inferior status at home or that his parents may actually be rejecting him. They also put the ball firmly back in the child's court in terms of solving the problem, which, given the child's immaturity and self-centeredness, he can hardly be expected to do.

Another common response to children's aggressive behavior is to increase the level of discipline. However, for the angry Disfavored child, this too only serves to confirm his sense of rejection. Punishing a child who already feels rejected is, at the very least, redundant. At worst, it can escalate the arguments the child has with his parents and other authority figures, and spur him to even more aggressive acts.

How to Deal with Peer Aggression

The Family Theory and Favoritism approach to peer aggression maintains that the angry child, who may be a bully or a gang member, is often one who is either feeling rejected or is actually rejected at home. The sense of being second best, of not being important, and of not belonging to the family fold is the main reason for this aggression. The child finds an outlet for his angry, vindictive feelings by harassing other children. *This aggressive behavior outside the home represents the child's attempt to gain the social power and status within a peer group that he couldn't get at home.*

The child's desire to attach herself to a peer group is a direct result of her lack of opportunity to become attached to the Prime Love-Giving parent at home. Sometimes this is because a competent PLG just isn't available, because the parent works very long hours or, more seriously, is a drug addict or an alcoholic. But often it occurs simply because a rival sibling is closer to the PLG, monopolizing this parent's attention and excluding the Disfavored, rebellious sibling.

This child then turns to the peer group as a way of validating herself and of acquiring self-confidence, pride, and social status. As a member of a group, she finally discovers the sense of belonging that is missing at home. This theory is borne out by statements made by youths who are members of gangs. They swear that *the peer group is their substitute family*, and that despite their aggression toward outsiders, *membership in the gang provides them with the mysterious feeling of belonging that they long for, but seem to lack at home*. To the gang member, his family stands in sharp contrast with his peer group, which gives him a great deal of attention, and where he feels both welcome and important.

Sadly, another characteristic of the aggressive child's burning rage is that it hardens the child to the pain of others. The pain of rejection by your own family is an extremely cutting and humiliating feeling that can leave you devastated. Whether real or imagined, the anger over rejection by your own family can be so acute, particularly for young people, that it blurs all sense of reality. It invades all of the child's thoughts and feelings, and touches her to such a degree that it alters her powers of reasoning and good judgment. The presence of such strongly felt anger also means that the child will probably remain emotionally immature and self-centered. In fact, in order to protect her interests, which she believes to be in jeopardy, she develops a powerful selfish bias in terms of the way she sees the rest of the world. *Self-pity* becomes the trademark of the child's personality, and *self-protection* her primary concern.

Given that the angry child has very little control over his behavior and his raw impulses have relatively free rein, the result can be the violent release of anger against unsuspecting victims, often his peers. The key to the angry child's apparent callousness lies in the fact that he feels the Prime Love-Giver is discriminating against him and depriving him of love. His immature reasoning goes like this: "If I'm so unloved at home and nobody cares about me, why should I care about how anyone else feels?" These children's self-centeredness always places their own interests first, making them incapable of putting themselves into someone else's shoes, particularly those of whoever is the true victim of their aggression. This was certainly true for both Lynn and Rita, who took advantage of their equal, Jackie.

Over time, the child's emotions freeze up and her anger against the outside world solidifies. She recedes into a self-indulgent way of thinking and behaving, and begins to view the world as one giant enemy, with herself as tiny and vulnerable. This view of themselves as *defenseless against a hostile world*, with the parallel quest for self-protection, is one that is echoed many times by members of teenage gangs.

On a much milder level than gang behavior, parents often find that many adolescents *conform slavishly to peer standards*. Some cling so steadfastly to their peer group that they neglect other, more worthwhile pursuits. They end up leaving school, smoking, taking drugs, or simply acting out for the joy of it. This kind of behavior is reinforced by the confidence they feel when they are with the other members of their group.

Once again, adults are left wondering why these children choose to follow the group's values rather than their parents'. And here again, Family Theory and Favoritism suggests that we look for feelings of rejection at home. Given that being a member of a teen gang or cult restores that vital sense of belonging for teenagers, it's a logical explanation for milder types of behavior too.

Peer Aggression in Adulthood

Salvatore owns a dress factory, and spends twelve hours a day at work. His employees are mainly immigrant women who are willing to work for less than the minimum wage. A few times a day, Salvatore makes the rounds on the factory floor. He often criticizes the women for not working fast enough, but this isn't the worst of it.

Checking up on the finished pieces, he invariably finds flaws. He then summons the woman responsible into his office—which always means trouble. In his position of power, he takes the liberty of making very personal and insulting attacks: "Do you have parents? Didn't they ever teach you that you have to work hard in order to live? What's your excuse for this lousy work?" Then he invades the more sensitive areas: "How many children do you have? Do you want them to starve?" He threatens her security:

"Maybe you think we're not treating you well enough here. Maybe you think you can get a better job somewhere else, eh?" Often, he ends up firing a woman on the spot for a minor error, just to set an example for the rest.

Adult aggression is a natural sequel to problems in adolescence. The adult who has a great deal of pent-up rage often intimidates other people. He may be unpredictable, look threatening, be in a bad mood much of the time, and use any excuse for an angry outburst. He may be emotionally or verbally abusive, use cutting criticism, shout at others, put them down, or otherwise make them feel miserable. An adult who expresses a great deal of uncontrolled aggression is usually characterized as a mean, nasty person whom other people find difficult to be around.

A common outlet for this explosive anger is in the person's private life, with the spouse and children. Inside the privacy of the home, verbal or physical threats easily cross over into open abuse. The full force of his anger is unleashed behind closed doors against the people who know him intimately and who are most likely to tolerate it. In many cases, through his well-honed social skill in hiding his aggression, an angry person presents a Dr. Jekyll and Mr. Hyde image. To the rest of the world, he often appears gentle and charming, but as soon as he gets home, he turns into a monster.

Anger can spread outside the family if the individual occupies a position of authority over others—as an employer, a teacher, or a member of the police force, for example. In these cases, the angry individual may take advantage of his position to be cruel to those who are in his charge, as Salvatore did on a regular basis with his employees. Yet Salvatore may well have been angry at home, too, since it is almost impossible to predict the specific area in which this aggression eventually finds its release.

Anger as Aggression Toward Parents and Other Authority Figures: *Rebellion*

Rhonda's family was fed up with her. From the time she was very small, she had always insisted on having her way. As a teen, she became involved with a group of girls who defied school rules by wearing unusual clothing. They also got tattooed, had their bodies pierced in numerous places, and wore a great deal of makeup. They were a loud bunch who made themselves known wherever they went.

One day, Rhonda's parents decided they'd had enough. They confronted her with her unruliness, which led to a big argument. To their dismay, however, nothing really changed. She still slept out a few nights a week, and would often come home drunk. From their perspective, the parents could see their daughter sliding down the slippery slope toward a life of drugs, prostitution, and crime. When they asked for a social worker to come to the house, Rhonda made sure she wasn't home.

Sadly, Rhonda moved out of the house a few weeks later to live on her own, and her parents haven't seen or heard from her in two years. But they have always been haunted by their guilt about being too harsh with her the day of that big confrontation.

An angry response to being Disfavored that is directed against parents is commonly known as *rebellion*. In our society, rebellion seems to peak in adolescence. It begins with the child opposing her parents' values and beliefs, and spreads to include new targets in the world at large. Eventually, any set of values can be singled out for challenge. A rebellious child might focus her anger on the education system, religion, the work ethic, the law, or society's values in general. The authority figures associated with these social structures—teachers, employers, police, social workers, lawyers, judges, and so on—are automatically attacked as well.

Sadly, there are many children in our society who leave the comfort of their homes for the cold of the streets because of the anger they bear toward their parents. In at least some of these cases, the reason for running away can be directly connected with feeling Disfavored at home. In one feature story I read in the *Toronto Star*, a sixteen-year-old girl named Melissa, who had lived on the street for two years, said of her parents: "They don't like me, they like my little sister. I am never, never going home." Other children are sometimes ejected from their homes because their parents, who haven't found successful ways of handling them and are exhausted, decide to impose Tough Love measures as a last-ditch stand against their children's persistent misbehavior.

It's normal, of course, for adolescents to make some attempt to separate themselves from the adults around them. Teenagers often dress in distinctly different ways, for instance, and adults usually tolerate this, sometimes even seeing it as an expression of their creativity. On the other hand, the adolescent who joins a group that not only dresses outrageously but also carries weapons and defies the police is giving out a stronger message than simply trying to be different. In this case, the bridge between creative self-expression and outright rebellion has been crossed. A highly rebellious attitude often involves the teenager becoming alienated from her family and aligning herself with the peer group instead, replacing her family's values with those of the group. Once rebellion is established as part of the child's personality and becomes her way of expressing her hostile feelings, it can no longer be considered just a passing phase.

How To Deal with Rebellion

> On a radio talk show, a woman was discussing her lovely, bright daughter who had slipped into a life of drugs and prostitution. "I'll never let her go," the mother said. "I'll follow her to the ends of the earth, and I'll always be there for her. No matter where she goes or what she does, she's still my daughter and she's my responsibility. Even if she falls apart, I'll be there to pick up the pieces."

145

Another woman said she felt the same sense of responsibility about her son, but since he had become involved with street gangs and violent behavior, she felt there was little she could do but wait until he was arrested.

As with sibling fighting, parents stand a much better chance of helping their child change if they address his underlying feelings of rejection, rather than ignoring his behavior or attempting to cope with individual problems as they come up. Left to fester on its own, rebellion can easily become worse with time, especially if the environment outside the family looks more inviting to the child and offers him rewards such as material goods, sexual gratification, drugs, or simply the excitement of hanging out with friends and feeling important.

All parents are braced for some form of rebellion from their adolescent children. It's an accepted fact of growing up. *But how is it that one child rebels while other siblings from the same family do not?* The nonrebellious teens have been raised in the same environment and with the same expectations as their delinquent sibling. Yet this happens in a large number of families: one child is actively defiant, while the other calmly sticks to the parents' values. Why are some children so susceptible to peer pressure, while others seem able to resist?

The difference can be easily explained in terms of Family Theory and Favoritism. Some children feel privileged, or Favored, at home, while others feel undermined, or Disfavored, by comparison. Children who feel Favored by their Prime Love-Giving parent identify with both their parents' and society's values, and are therefore reluctant to join in antisocial activities. *The love connection between the Favored child and the PLG means the child aligns himself with adult values. And this relationship is far more important than any acceptance or social status that a peer group might offer.*

In contrast with the Favored child, the Disfavored child's rebellion reflects her unhappiness with her home situation. Because they don't feel accepted at home, Disfavored children may turn their anger first against their parents and then against other authority figures. Regularly misbehaving around their parents is the first warning sign of a growing sense of opposition to the world. As the boundaries of their rebellion grow larger, angry Disfavored children may challenge any authority figures who get in their way. Their discontent makes them susceptible to an antisocial lifestyle and, depending on the child's neighborhood and economic status, it's not surprising to find that these children eventually become involved in crime, prostitution, or drugs.

For the child who falls into this kind of life, the future is unpredictable. Once the teenager has become deeply involved in any or all of these habits—perhaps even to the point of being arrested—there is often a limit to what parents can do. They usually have to rely on social agencies to intervene and help in rehabilitating their child. Since the child has deliberately rejected her family and has chosen to align herself with her peers, she is likely to refuse her parents' help and reject their attempts at reconciliation. Hurt pride will often lead her to insist that her parents "just don't understand," that they never liked her anyway and that she will do much better without them.

However, it is certain—as in the example of the mother who said she would follow her daughter to the ends of the earth—that some contact with a child in trouble is usually better than none at all, and that parents should try to *maintain their offers of love to a child who has gone astray.* At the same time, they must also try to accept the fact that, at this point in her life, the child has found other ways to gratify her needs, whether monetary, chemical, sexual, or social. These new ties were formed to replace the old ones with family members, and aren't easily broken.

To bolster their courage, parents should remember that *the child's ultimate fantasy will always involve being loved by both parents, and especially being the exclusive love object of the Prime Love-Giver.* The child still depends on his parents' love and approval, whatever he might say. Even at this advanced stage of rebellion, loving their child is the single greatest contribution that parents can make toward helping him.

In some sad cases, parents might continue to reject a child regardless of whether he improves his behavior. It then becomes important for the child to deal with the profound feelings of loss that come from knowing he was never loved by his parents and perhaps never will be. The ways in which these feelings of rejection can be dealt with are discussed in Chapter 12, under "Dealing with Feelings of Disfavor as an Adult."

9

Depression, Anxiety and Other Reactions to Disfavor

Depression As a Reaction to Disfavor

The biography of Princess Grace of Monaco tells the story of the success (or image of success) of a girl who was sadly and overwhelmingly Disfavored by both her parents. As the third of four siblings, Grace's secondary position was made most clear by her father, who constantly underestimated her capabilities. He favored her firstborn sister Peggy above all the other children, and then Kell, the second-born and only son. Her fourth-born sister, Lizanne, was also loved and spoiled as the baby of the family.

Grace herself was berated and ignored by all the family, craving the attention of any of her siblings who would offer it. Tragically, she seems to have spent most of her young life trying to appease and ingratiate herself with other family members, all of whom were extroverted except for her. Shy and retiring, she seems to have played the classic Cinderella role. Lonely and isolated, some say she was closest with the black household butler, who became her greatest friend and confidant. Others maintain that the greatest influence in her life came from her paternal uncle George, who first introduced her to the theatre.

Ironically, Grace Kelly's finest qualities—"her self-containment, her quiet poise and her air of refinement," which are described by author Sarah Bradford as her most feminine and ladylike traits—probably most accurately reflected her deep depression and her wounded self-image as a young girl.

Besides the angry reaction to Disfavor, which was discussed in the previous chapter, the second form of expression of a Disfavored child's feelings of rivalry is *depression*.

Depression, the deepest form of sadness, reflects the child's grief at having lost a major life struggle—the struggle with a rival sibling for the love of their Prime Love-Giving parent. This fundamental feeling of loss and personal failure, which is at the root of *all* reactions to Disfavor, has a powerful bearing on the child's self-esteem. As loved as a child may be in reality, it is the child's *feeling that she is loved less than a rival sibling* that has the potential to diminish her sense of self-worth, a fact that was certainly true in Grace Kelly's case.

The First Stage: Extreme Shyness

Lack of self-worth can translate into a growing sadness in the child. In one of its mildest forms, this sadness may be manifested as simple shyness. To a certain degree, some shyness or social reticence is part of a child's normal, healthy development. It's helpful for every child to acquire some self-restraint, along with the ability to be reflective, introspective, and self-critical. Certainly it is in society's interests to encourage a reluctance to encroach on other people's privacy and property.

In the very sad individual, however, *shyness and self-restraint are taken to an extreme.* Such a person is not only socially inhibited but often actively avoids being with others. He may retreat from a crowd, seem socially awkward, or have to be coaxed to become involved in activities outside his immediate, familiar environment. You should become concerned about your child if shyness prevents him from leading an ordinary social life, playing with friends or developing appropriate relationships. Eleanor Roosevelt's life provides a good example:

> Eleanor Roosevelt had a happy upbringing for the first few years of her life. As the firstborn daughter of a well-to-do family, she was very close to her father, who treated her as his "greatest treasure." However, soon after he married, he embarked on a reckless lifestyle of drinking and drugs, and was away from home for much of his daughter's childhood.
>
> Eleanor's mother, although she was home, seems to have been an immature, self-interested person who spent very little time with her daughter. Eleanor pined for her mother, even though she lived under the same roof. By the time Eleanor was five, she was apparently such a sad and worried child that her mother tauntingly nicknamed her "Little Granny." Her next-youngest brother, Ellie, was born about that time, but we have little knowledge about his short life.
>
> Over the next three years, Eleanor lost her mother, her brother Ellie and her beloved father, though it is reported that she hardly reacted at all to the loss of her mother. She and her youngest brother, Hall, went to live with their maternal grandmother. Eleanor remained very shy, self-conscious, and prudish, and, until she married, thought of herself as an "ugly duckling."

Excessive shyness reflects the child's conviction that others don't like her. As a Disfavored child who feels rejected by her immediate family, she comes to believe that people outside the family don't value her either. Eventually, she concludes that they might be right, that she isn't worth much as a person. As these negative feelings grow roots and permeate her personality, she makes a habit of avoiding other people.

The Second Stage: Social Withdrawal

The stage is set for *social withdrawal*, the next step toward more severe depression. Social withdrawal is a more serious expression of the same sense of personal inadequacy that underlies simple shyness. Someone who is shy still has the basic *desire* to stay in contact with other people. A person who is socially withdrawn, however, isolates himself and *actively avoids* others. His sense of worthlessness becomes so profound that it alters his fundamental human need to be with other people. Benny Hill is a good example of this—a man who built such a reclusive lifestyle for himself that it was difficult for others to get to know him at all. Although he was both famous and well-liked, he socialized very little and never married.

The Third Stage: Depression

The most extreme form of sadness is full-blown *depression*. You might suspect a child is depressed if she goes about her normal day-to-day activities with unusual slowness or is extremely cautious and restrained. Refusing to talk is another way that a depressed child insulates herself from the outside world. By withdrawing verbally from her environment, the child envelops herself in a safe, internal world where she doesn't run the risk of suffering verbal assaults. Constant daydreaming is another clue to a child's feelings of deep sadness. Through daydreams, she attempts to cope with what she sees as her lack of power in the real world by imagining herself as important and influential. It is said of Grace Kelly, for example, that when she was once locked in a closet by her younger sister, she went unnoticed for several hours because she was so busy playing make-believe with her dolls.

One of the most common, though least understood, manifestations of childhood depression is *lack of motivation*. An unmotivated child expresses his depression through a lack of interest in most subjects and activities. Rather than demonstrating an enthusiasm for life, the depressed child seems to be gripped by a pessimism that stops him from believing that anything could be exciting.

Lack of motivation is particularly obvious at school, of course. Parents and educators see many a bright child who not only shows no interest in academics but also refuses to take advantage of any offers of help. Such a child baffles and frustrates adults, who tend to fixate on the child's apparent intransigence and accuse him of laziness, as happened with Winston Churchill when he was young. Both teachers and parents usually resort to nagging, taunting, or imposing extra discipline in the hope of spurring the child into action. Sometimes we might think that the belligerent or yelling approach works well, as it did in Margaret Halsey's case. You may recall that she skipped two grades and maintained a 99 percent average thanks to her father's strict demands. In the end, however, Margaret did suffer from the effects of this verbal pressure: she became an alcoholic and lost custody of her only child.

In most cases, a depressed, unmotivated child simply stonewalls his parents and other authority figures rather than caving in to their demands. Faced with what he sees as a threat—produce good results, or else—he might say, "I don't want to play basketball—it's a stupid game!" Or, "I won't take piano lessons—you're the only parent who tries to force their kid to play music!"

As well as digging in his heels and refusing to do as he is asked, the depressed child will often counterattack, believing that the best defense is offense. The child's defensive response is designed *to avoid exposure to the possibility of failure* at all costs. The child might challenge her parents—"You can't make me do my homework"—or go to her room and do nothing.

Unfortunately, the child's refusal to cooperate only helps fuel the adult's negative attitude toward him—those lurking feelings of Disfavor. These feelings are continually reaffirmed when, in the back of their minds, adults inadvertently compare this child with other, more studious children. Film star Michael Landon is a good example of a depressed, Disfavored child whose grades fell drastically as he entered high school:

> When Michael Landon was born, three and a half years after his sister Evelyn, he says she called him ugly, and the name "Ugy" stuck. Born Eugene Orowitz of a Jewish father and a Catholic mother, Michael knew that his mother

strongly favored his sister, whom she saw as the best prospect for Broadway stardom. He was a straight-A student in grade school, but a loner and full of fears. When he didn't outgrow his bed-wetting, his parents teased and humiliated him by hanging the wet sheets out for all to see.

When Michael got to high school, his grades slipped badly. He remembers himself as an outcast who was left to stand alone against his family, and against the whole world. He finally got involved in javelin-throwing, which became his lifeline, but his parents weren't enthusiastic and never came to watch or support him. They were shocked when he got a sports scholarship to a good university.

Landon wrote an autobiographical screenplay for a film called *Sam's Son* and financed it himself. Although it wasn't successful, he embarked on the project with the hope of helping children who felt as lost and lonely as he did when he was growing up.

Whatever the outcome of the aggressive approach to the unmotivated child—whether she shapes up or continues to do nothing—it's certain that she can end up paying a staggering emotional price. If you apply Family Theory and Favoritism, though, it's clear that the child's lack of motivation and pessimism masks an underlying feeling of low self-esteem and fear of failure. Excuses and verbal defenses are intended to cover up this low level of confidence.

Deep down, *most children know about their feelings of rivalry*. The problem is that they're too embarrassed to communicate them. They fear that their feelings might be trivialized by their parents (which they often are). They're too proud to admit they feel so unhappy because of the loss of love from their prime parent that they can hardly function. They're frightened by the prospect of being made fun of by their parents and other family members, as in Michael Landon's case, and they're thoroughly ashamed of being second-best.

When these feelings are hidden, repressed, or ignored, the potential to sink into depression becomes a real possibility. Many children, especially adolescents, can deceive their caregivers—and perhaps even themselves—by keeping their depression and its real source well hidden. Gradually, however, they lose their sense of hope, purpose and optimism, even though they're making every effort to maintain a normal façade.

Parents are often very surprised when one of their children, who seems to have been getting along marvelously, suddenly begins to show signs of deep-rooted depression. Outwardly, the child seems to have all the talents necessary for success and has a lot to live for. But if the parents were to delve into the depressed child's psyche, they would discover that she feels she is struggling merely to keep afloat. Even when there is no obvious reason for distress, she still seems to feel a mysterious sense of pressure that may be completely incomprehensible to adults. But it's all too familiar to the depressed child, who can end up being entirely overwhelmed by this feeling of desperation. It seems the child feels that she *has to wage a constant war, but never has the chance of winning.*

Many children turn to drugs or alcohol in an attempt to relieve this inexplicable pressure—the sensation of never measuring up, of being a "loser." Mind-altering substances provide both an avenue of escape and a means of self-destruction. At the most tragic extreme, if the child loses all hope of ever gaining personal recognition, his sense of purpose in life begins to fade. At this point, thoughts of giving up the battle and ending his life begin to invade his mind, and may look like a realistic solution to his problems. To the depressed person, death may even be regarded as attractive. Consider the case of Ruth Bell Graham:

> A deeply religious girl at a very early age, Ruth would pray to the Lord every night. In her prayers, she would ask the Almighty to let her die for Him. Her depressive mood not only found its expression in the form of a deep spirituality, but also spread to include a sincere sympathy for all creatures, both alive and dead.
>
> When she went to boarding school, Ruth had a very hard time adjusting. She cried a great deal and isolated herself

from her schoolmates. Her parents, always keenly interested in her welfare, became concerned about the fact that she was spending so much time writing letters home, which hardly seemed to leave her time to do anything else. Worried about the mournful tone of her letters, they wrote to the headmaster to notify him that they recognized their daughter's tendencies "to revel in the sad side of things" and realized that their daughter had allowed her religion to take "a slightly morbid turn."

On one occasion, in conversation with a friend, Ruth was overheard declaring her joy at the thought that the end of the world might come soon, and they could all go to Heaven.

Most children who contemplate death, of course, do so in anguish, not anticipation. Besides their profound sense of sadness, they often express in suicide notes the feeling of *a never-ending struggle* and their battle to overcome it: "I can't go on like this. It hurts too much inside."

Whatever the severity of the depressed child's reaction, the uninformed adult is inevitably left wondering: "Who is she waging this bitter war against? Why is she so withdrawn?" "What pain is he trying to hide by drinking and taking drugs? And who could be responsible for placing so much mental strain on him that he would even contemplate suicide?"

Using a Favoritism perspective, it is easy to see the powerful connection between childhood depression and the low self-esteem that comes from feeling Disfavored, or second best, at home. *At its deepest level, the sibling struggle is related to every child's sense of purpose in life.* The depressed child's thoughts are filled both by the negative self-image that comes from being Disfavored and by a sense of *betrayal*. The child's reasoning goes like this: "If I lost the battle with my sibling and he's obviously loved more than me, then I am not lovable at all. Somebody took away the love that should have been mine." It is this additional feeling of having been betrayed by those who are closest to her, and should have been responsible for loving her that overwhelms her.

Depression in a Disfavored child also has to do with the feeling that he is somehow *personally responsible* for this loss. The child's reasoning continues: "I am not a worthwhile person because I couldn't manage to get the love I needed so badly. I'm totally disappointed in myself because I failed." The key here is the child's sense of *failure* in the battle that, from his perspective, is the most important one in life.

Although the dynamics of depression are at best hazy and elusive, understanding how important the sibling struggle is for children can help us cope with our children's sometimes mysterious depressions and behavior patterns, traces of which are likely to affect them for the rest of their lives. Using a Family Theory and Favoritism perspective significantly enhances our insight into these dynamics.

Anxiety as a Reaction to Disfavor

Anxiety is the third type of response to being Disfavored, next to anger and depression. Here is an example of a famous star whose anxiety about her position of Disfavor colored her whole life.

> In spite of her brilliant acting and singing career, Barbra Streisand's personal life has been marked by fear, insecurity, and self-seclusion. Her father died when she was only one year old, leaving her mother sad, emotionally withdrawn, and worried about supporting Barbra and her eight-year-old brother, Sheldon. Barbra's family moved in with her grandparents who, though they were decent people, were emotionally distant and inclined to be very strict with the children.
>
> Barbra tried to get her mother's attention by pretending to be sick, refusing to eat, and even faking asthma attacks. She was always an A student, but seemingly this wasn't enough to please her mother, who often reminded her that she was not a particularly pretty girl. When Barbra was seven, her

mother remarried, but acquiring a stepfather made her even more anxious about failing to get her mother's love.

Anxiety as a reaction to Disfavor can be responsible for general personality traits, such as immaturity, poor reasoning, or worrying, or it can be the cause of more specific behavior, such as nail-biting and hyperactivity. Only some of the ways in which children or adults express anxiety will be discussed here, since the list is so long that it defies complete coverage.

Nightmares are one of the most obvious clues to anxiety. Feelings of fear that are barely noticeable during the day can spring forth at night. Usually, the nightmare's principal theme involves either being abandoned or being harmed in some way. In a child's dream world, this fear is often represented as a direct physical threat, such as being chased by a monster who wants to eat or kill its helpless victim. In reality, the threat is usually not physical but psychological. *The child has a crushing fear of being overcome by a more powerful person in his immediate environment—the rival sibling—and thus losing the love of the Prime Love-Giver.*

Phobias are a similar type of anxiety-based reaction in which a child or adult attaches her feelings of fear to specific creatures, factors, or activities, such as spiders, heights, darkness, or flying. The child's panic at the thought of going to school is a common childhood phobia. This reaction stems from the child's fear that she might lose her connection with the Prime Love-Giver if this precious person's love disappears or is claimed by another sibling while the child is out of the house.

A *preoccupation with perfection* is an extremely common expression of anxiety. A Disfavored person's obsession with perfection sometimes starts at a very early age, and may be particularly visible in his efforts to be a perfect student. School is a fertile area for competition, since the child can strive for perfection by getting top marks. However, unlike the expression of most anxieties, applying the competitive struggle to intellectual or academic performance can be a very positive way of expressing sibling rivalry.

It might seem surprising that the child who becomes a teacher's pet or who usually brings home a straight-A report card, like Barbra Streisand

and Michael Landon, often feels Disfavored at home. But by now, you can probably figure out why this is. Once again, the child is competing against his sibling for first place in the Prime Love-Giver's affections. By obtaining near-perfect grades, the child frequently succeeds in getting the PLG's positive attention. Most adults praise a child who is doing well at school, and this effectively allows the child to win back at least some love and praise, as well as providing him with some leverage to challenge the Favored sibling.

An adult's perfectionism can affect any area of her life. A perfectionist can make a highly efficient worker, and can end up with significant professional success. On the other hand, a perfectionist can also become a workaholic, with all the neglect of family and friends that implies.

A perfectionist who runs a household and is raising children may become obsessed with performing the household tasks as perfectly as possible. Organizing the family by constantly checking times, places, and events is also typical of this kind of person.

Unfortunately, the perfectionist's need for tidiness, order, and cleanliness can—and often does—intrude on the lives of the other family members. Striving for perfection is an attempt to deal with anxiety by exerting as much control as possible over daily events, but at the same time it often leads to controlling other people's lives and behavior as well. The perfectionist often demands that her spouse and children improve their performance too, which means that they are also affected by the parent's anxiety. Joan Rivers' story about her mother is a good example of how this kind of behavior can affect the whole family. Joan's mother was determined that her daughters would learn how to eat according to strict rules of etiquette—when to use the right spoon, the right fork, and so on—so that they could behave properly in a restaurant. This turned out to be one of the great hurdles in Joan's life. She laughs when she looks back on it now, but to her younger self, this felt like a meaningless exercise that merely destroyed everybody's feeling of comfort at home.

There are countless other ways in which the Disfavored child can express her anxiety. She may regress to sucking her thumb, revert to baby talk, or wet the bed, as May Gruber and Michael Landon did. The anxious Disfavored child may whine, cry easily, or cling to the Prime Love-Giver. Or he may express chronic unhappiness and constantly reject whatever his parents or teachers have to offer. He may appear restless and agitated, or may constantly seek attention. An adult who was Disfavored as a child may be unable to focus his attention on a single career, a particular social group, or a single spouse. He may stick religiously to schedules or strict regimes, or resist changes of any sort.

Other general reactions to anxiety include a host of *physical symptoms* that can be stress-related, such as headaches or stomach aches. Anxiety can, in fact, be so powerful that the child or adult experiences real medical symptoms, such as allergies, asthma, or skin conditions. Other well-known physical symptoms of anxiety are eating disorders—anorexia, bulimia, and obesity. These particular ailments are often combined with a powerful, underlying depression, in which eating—or not eating—is the expression of a deep-rooted death wish.

Finally, anxiety combined with uncontrollable anger can be expressed as a *temper tantrum*. Even though parents might think otherwise, tantrums generally aren't directed at the parents themselves or other specific targets, but are the child's clumsy attempts to attract people's attention, sympathy, and love.

From a Family Theory and Favoritism point of view, the Disfavored child's anxiety stems from her reaction to the thought of being *abandoned*, especially by the Prime Love-Giver, or of being harmed in some way by outside forces if the PLG is absent. In fact, feeling Disfavored stems in part from feeling *insecure*, because as far as the Disfavored child is concerned, she isn't receiving the love she feels is rightly hers. This insecurity leads, in turn, to a lack of confidence about the future.

Above all, the Disfavored child is constantly anxious that he will lose—or is actually losing—the battle for the PLG's love. A Disfavored child's nightmares provide particular insight into how real this sense of danger is for him. Indeed, the killer monsters that often populate his dreams show that the child believes losing the PLG's love is the same as losing his connection with life itself.

Like Barbra Streisand, who remains a perfectionist as an adult, the Disfavored child's quest for perfection is rooted in her lack of self-esteem. Receiving only a small part of the PLG's attention compared to her sibling, her self-criticism becomes so dominant that nothing she does seems good enough to her, and no amount of effort is enough to retrieve the PLG's lost love.

Other Reactions to Disfavor

Besides the three main categories of emotional response to Disfavor—anger, depression, and anxiety—there are some general traits that tend to characterize the Disfavored child's personality.

Mistrust is an important undercurrent of feeling that often goes along with Disfavor. It begins when the Disfavored child suspects that the Favored child experiences more closeness and warmth with the Prime Love-Giver than she does. This feeling of suspicion, which starts within the Circle of Love, eventually spreads to other relationships outside the family.

A child demonstrates lack of trust by misbehaving, defying authority, or withdrawing. Dealing with the mistrustful Disfavored child can quickly become a tug-of-war—everyone tries to convince the child to do a certain thing, but the child has other ideas. The mistrust soon becomes mutual, and parents begin to think, "Why does this child constantly oppose us, when we've done everything we possibly can to be good to her? Besides," they go on to themselves, "how can we be bad parents when our other children seem to trust us and don't behave so provocatively?" The parents begin not only to lose confidence in the child but also to stop placing much faith in their relationship with her. A wall is built and a rift develops between parents and child, and the contrast with the Favored sibling becomes more glaring than ever.

If it's not dealt with in childhood, a lack of trust can become deeply embedded in the Disfavored adult's personality. He may be suspicious of other people, checking up on them or continually asking questions to make sure that he's not being tricked. Or he may be argumentative and uncompromising. By taking issue with other people's competence or intentions and insisting on his own way, the mistrustful Disfavored person tries to control the situation in order to increase his sense of security.

Feeling cheated and betrayed is also typical of the Disfavored individual. Think of a group of children taking turns at jumping rope. Each child gets the same number of chances to jump, but one child insists on an extra turn. When the other children say no, the child argues, tries to bully her friends into agreeing, and eventually steps into the middle of the rope to stop the game entirely. The child also refuses to take a turn holding the end of the rope. Eventually, her behavior makes everybody so unhappy that the game is spoiled. But had she been given the extra turn she wanted, the story would most likely have been the same. It wouldn't have been long before her anger would have erupted in another way, and she would have found another excuse to be disruptive.

What lies behind this behavior is a deep-rooted sense of having been cheated in the game of life. Regardless of the actual circumstances, the Disfavored individual constantly feels *he's entitled to more than he's getting.* His competitive or defiant behavior is a product of *this general state of anger, which has accumulated in response to feeling betrayed.* The child (or adult) is trying to compensate for his lost social position as the Favored child and his humiliation at being defeated by his rival brother or sister. Retaliation for this supposed injustice is unpredictable. It is directed outward, but sometimes a specific person is the target and sometimes, as in the case of the skipping game, everyone is made to suffer.

Self-centeredness, or outright *selfishness*, is also typical of Disfavored people. As we discussed in an earlier chapter, self-centeredness is left over from our primitive instincts to defend our property and territory against the intrusion of others. The Disfavored child may seem to consider no one but himself. Grabbing and hoarding toys or other possessions are both common symptoms of Disfavor.

Arguing with the self-centered child is usually futile. After a while, a parent can start to believe that the child actually enjoys putting her parents through the useless exercise of pleading for common sense. And to some degree, the parent is right. The child's unreasonable behavior is, in part, a way for her to vent her anger toward the parent. However, her selfishness also reflects her self-centered way of thinking, which has become a part of her attitude toward the world. This need to protect her own interests against a seemingly hostile world exerts a definite influence on the child's behavior, and may continue to do so well into adulthood. Not having developed enough trust to believe that her needs will be willingly filled by others, the Disfavored child may believe she has to resort to lying, cheating, or stealing in order to defend her rights.

The *intelligence* of a child may be profoundly affected by feeling Disfavored. The ability to exercise good, clear judgment and to listen to reason is vitally dependent on the state of a child's emotions. Because anger, sadness, and anxiety fill the Disfavored child's mind, there is a strong chance that these emotions will interfere with her intellectual development. Normally, self-centered thinking decreases significantly by the time a child reaches adolescence. A teenager is capable of imagining other people's realities and feelings, and can logically think her way through a problem. However, in the immature Disfavored child, self-centered thinking dominates her mind far beyond an appropriate age. Her ongoing selfishness means she will be late in acquiring the ability to think logically or dispassionately, a factor that makes any reasonable discussion with the child difficult, if not at times impossible.

Poor judgment is particularly obvious when the Disfavored child is around a peer group or joins in gang activities. The child may follow up on a senseless dare, challenge the police, or otherwise behave recklessly in an effort to gain the attention and acceptance of his peers and to get that desired feeling of belonging that we discussed in the previous chapter.

For adults, who have their own well-defined standards when it comes to evaluating children, *the angry Disfavored child can easily appear to be intellectually deficient.* For one thing, part of the child's rebellion often involves using sloppy or downright rude language, which contributes to the impression of low intelligence. For another, adults tend to assume a child is not particularly smart if she argues with them constantly, using dead-end disagreements: "Why did you hit your little brother?" "Because he's dumb!" Or, "Why are you causing trouble in school?" "Because school is stupid! Nobody knows anything!"

But like the excuse of bad heredity, jumping to conclusions about the low intelligence of Disfavored children is just one more way of rationalizing the child's bad behavior. It reflects adults' frustration as they try to figure out the source of the child's actions as well as try to put their own unsettling relationship with the child into some kind of perspective.

Immaturity is one of the strongest signs of Disfavor. When a child appears immature, you can bet that her negative feelings from being Disfavored are interfering with her social, emotional, and possibly intellectual development. In a small child, this may mean the child regresses to babyish behavior. An older child may remain too dependent on adults, be socially isolated, or otherwise behave in ways that aren't appropriate for her age. Again, you'll tend to see poor social judgment and faulty reasoning, rooted in the child's self-centered attitude. And again, low self-esteem is at the core of the Disfavored child's resistance to maturity. This seems to have been true in the case of Phil Donahue:

> American talk-show host Phil Donahue says of his relationship with his sister Kathy, five years younger than him, that they "functioned in separate universes." Yet he must have felt the pinch of Disfavor, since he became a very combative kid. Though he wasn't really tough, and was actually quite afraid inside, he speculates that he tried to fight off his fear by exposing himself to head-on fights with the biggest bullies. His preoccupation with his emotions must have consumed a great deal of his energy, for in his autobiography he openly admits: "Now, at age 43, I am curious about this behavior and have more than a passing interest in understanding it."
>
> Donahue performed poorly at college. In an interview with one of the head priests at the college, he self-effacingly offered the explanation that his problem was "immaturity," to which the good Father, not to be taken in by this ploy, responded that the "immaturity" was nobody's fault but his own.

Verbal and social manipulation are by far the most acceptable, refined, and institutionalized ways of expressing anger toward the outside world. In fact, *the great majority of the population uses socially manipulative tactics once they reach adulthood.* In their mildest forms, these kinds of manipulation can be interesting, stimulating, and entertaining. However, they can also incorporate a certain amount of anger that can be subtle and difficult to identify. This anger is evident in malicious gossip, plotting, telling lies, being sneaky, putting other people down, speaking sharply, using other people to one's advantage, and controlling and dominating other people's lives.

Sometimes, there is only a fine moral line between using mild social manipulation legitimately, as a way of advancing yourself professionally or socially, and using it unfairly. Some typical dubious manipulative strategies include not telling the whole truth, deliberately misleading others, and taking advantage of a trusting relationship. This unscrupulous kind of manipulation can also involve using one's charm to dupe people in order to climb up the social or professional ladder.

People who have the gift of the gab can often manipulate others and win them over to their point of view. They use words to comfort, flatter, entertain or convince. The social manipulator might appear to have a great deal more knowledge, intelligence, or sincerity than he actually possesses, and through his skill with words, may persuade others to trust him. Thus, a politician might make promises that she has no intention of carrying out, or a man or woman might pursue a mate solely for the sake of wealth or professional status.

Money is a powerful motivating force for many Disfavored adults, who often cling to material possessions as a replacement for the love they feel they lost in their childhood battle with their rival sibling. Accumulating wealth seems to fill the compelling need for security and power that many Disfavored people experience.

By the same token, Disfavored people often have a very strong *competitive drive*. They are inclined to see others, especially their peers, as potential rivals, and the intense desire to outdo them is reminiscent of their first battle with the Favored sibling. Jealousy—of other people's achievements and possessions—is a potent motivator. The Disfavored person's competitive streak can be expressed through school work, aggressive business practices, sports, or acquiring more material goods. Each new challenge is a constant reminder of that childhood trauma—the loss and failure that the Disfavored child experienced in her family of origin.

The Positive Effects of Being Disfavored

Finally, *it would be wrong to assume that to be Favored is all good and to be Disfavored is all bad.* After all, according to Family Theory and Favoritism, at least half of the population is probably Disfavored.

In fact, being Disfavored can have distinctly positive effects. Some children, because they feel Disfavored, learn to compete vigorously and to set high standards of achievement for themselves. When the Disfavored person's competitive drive is translated into the pursuit of excellence or other ambitions such as accumulating assets, the results can be highly rewarding. Because a child is Disfavored, she may be spurred to much greater heights than a Favored sibling. This was certainly true for such people as Roseanne Barr, Simone de Beauvoir, and Barbra Streisand, as well as for Alfred Adler and Rudolf Dreikurs, both of whom became accomplished psychological theorists. And as we all know, our society respects individuals who achieve high academic goals, notable wealth, or significant career goals.

In fairness, you should also remember that being raised as a Favored child has its drawbacks too, and certainly doesn't guarantee success or happiness in life, as we will discuss further in Chapter 10. Given their sense of entitlement, Favored people tend to become more upset by minor setbacks than Disfavored people, who have already learned to cope with feelings of failure. And because Favored people are less socially shrewd than their Disfavored counterparts, other people can more easily take advantage of them. Finally, the envy the Favored child sometimes feels from family members—both from the other siblings and from the Auxiliary Love-Giver—is in itself cause for intense grief and suffering.

As you'll see in Chapter 11, the remedy for Disfavor is a form of affirmative action, performed by the parents on behalf of the Disfavored child. By adopting a positive attitude toward their Disfavored child and slightly loosening the ties with their Favored one, parents can do no harm, and certainly stand to gain a great deal, since this simple adjustment in parental attitude has a very good chance of working to the advantage of all concerned.

10

The Favored Personality

So far, we've talked about Disfavored people, both children and adults, and the ways in which anger, depression, and anxiety affect their personality development. Now you might ask: How does a typical Favored person behave?

To begin with, anyone who was a Favored child is usually more free of the anger, depression, and anxiety that often plague adults who were Disfavored as children. This is because children who were Favored as they were growing up felt a deep-seated security about their connection with the Prime Love-Giver, rather than experiencing the Disfavored child's constant disappointment in this regard. Consequently, *Favored people are generally more satisfied with their lot in life*, which affects the way they behave and contributes to an overall positive, optimistic attitude. The following brief biographical description is typical.

> Famed tenor Luciano Pavarotti was not only the favorite of his family, but of the entire neighborhood in the town of Modena, Italy, where he was raised. His family always treated him as more important than his sister Gabriella, five years younger, who had little say in family affairs. And on top of that, he was lucky to be the youngest and only boy in the immediate area. The fact that everyone doted on him made him "a tiny superstar."

While his parents worked, Pavarotti stayed with his grandmother, who adored him and rarely disciplined him. Looking back on it, he felt privileged to have had such a blissful childhood in which he lived every day as it came and experienced time as never-ending.

As a young man, Pavarotti seems to have been "more spirited and full of life" than his friends. When it became clear that he had a great singing career ahead of him, his family did whatever they could to encourage him, providing him with moral support and as much financial support as they could afford.

Now a fully fledged star, Pavarotti describes himself as somewhat naive and trusting, and admits to having "an undeniably earthy side" to his personality. He says he is optimistic and enthusiastic, and puts his whole heart into everything he does.

Favored children can grow up to be *people-pleasers* who thrive on the prospect of making others happy. In fact, Favored individuals are often *people-oriented.* They tend to be sociable, enjoy intimacy, and are relatively relaxed and easygoing. In their dealings with others, they are frequently kind, patient, and warm.

Thanks to their generous nature, it is common for the Favored adult to enjoy children. An interesting question is whether Favored people make better Prime Love-Givers than Disfavored people. In fact, in the complicated dynamics of real life, Favored people don't necessarily become PLGs to their own children. Nor, for that matter, do they necessarily do a better job of parenting than Disfavored people.

Favored children usually *adopt their parents' and society's values.* Because they grew up in a close, loving relationship with their Prime Love-Giver, Favored children become powerfully connected with the adult world at an early age. Their habits, standards of behavior, and ways of communicating are copied directly from the adult model.

Favored children are thus *less likely to deviate from adult codes of behavior.*

This means they're less likely to challenge their parents' values or to rebel during their adolescence. They're also not as inclined to join a cult or gang, take drugs, or indulge in other kinds of acting out that adults find unacceptable. Backed by a solid value system and their own self-confidence, they are less vulnerable to their peers' judgment and opinions.

Many Favored individuals possess *good verbal skills*. Like their value system, this ability comes from their strong connection with the Prime Love-Giver. Favored children often mimic adult styles of speech. The ability to talk and present yourself well in society is part of the Favored child's attempt to copy adult behavior. If a Favored child develops good verbal skills, she will appear more intelligent and *socially mature* at a younger age than a Disfavored child. Favored children's tendency to develop better verbal skills, combined with adopting their parents' values, means that they attract positive attention and are more likable to adults, which in turn solidifies their Favored position.

Adult values, good verbal skills, a liking for children, and the privilege of making others happy are combined in this description of the life of comedian Bill Cosby:

> The essence of Bill Cosby's personality is captured in the very first lines of his biography. Bill's mother, Anna Cosby, is quoted as saying, "The only thing I had to give him was plenty of love, and oh . . . I gave him all I had."
>
> As the firstborn in a very poor family, Bill was the apple of his mother's eye. Unfortunately, his father was an alcoholic who eventually abandoned the family. His brother James, two years younger, died of rheumatic fever at the age of six, and another brother was epileptic.
>
> When Bill was eleven, he took a job as a shoe-shine boy, using an old orange crate for a stand. He became his mother's right-hand man, doing odd jobs to help her support the family. Any spare time he had was demanded by his two younger brothers, whom he parented in place of their missing father, and who developed a great deal of respect for him.

Perhaps because of his nature, formed as a Favored child, Cosby seems to have been able to draw some benefits from these hard times. He believes the main reason he resisted the temptation to join his peers in stealing and making trouble was that he felt, if he were put in prison, there would be nobody to look after his mother. In truth, Cosby seems to have cherished his mother above anyone else, and she obviously felt the same way about him.

Favored people are often *less controlling* than Disfavored individuals. They don't have the same need to organize and regulate events, and are less anxious about planning ahead. Since the Favored person doesn't feel compelled to know what will happen next, she can be flexible and can more easily accommodate unforeseen eventualities. While the Disfavored person might demand a precise schedule, the Favored individual will tend to be quite happy to let events unfold as they may. By the same token, Favored people are less troubled by anxiety, perfectionism, and obsessive worrying about the future.

Money is not usually important to a Favored person. The drive to amass money or other material goods isn't high on most Favored people's list of priorities, and certainly isn't as significant as it is for someone who was Disfavored as a child. For the Disfavored sibling, this powerful desire to acquire money or material goods is rooted in the insecurities of his position in the family of origin. Lacking such insecurities, the Favored person has less need to shore up his self-worth with possessions or cash.

On the other hand, the Favored person would put a high priority on having something for the sake of its sentimental value. In fact, a Favored person's general philosophy includes more emphasis on personal feelings and less on achieving goals merely for the sake of winning or accumulating assets.

Favoritism and High Achievement

According to Birth Order Theory, the firstborn child almost always ends up as the high achiever in a family. And if a person is firstborn and a high achiever, it would be easy to assume that she is Favored as well.

However, remember that the term Favored has a very specific meaning—it refers to *the child's emotional connection with a Prime Love-Giving parent, as compared with a Disfavored sibling*. Rudolf Dreikurs and Simone de Beauvoir are both examples of firstborn high achievers who, despite their academic abilities, were nonetheless Disfavored thanks to being displaced from their initial positions of Favor by their younger siblings. Dreikurs talks passionately of his dethronement by his impish younger sister, while de Beauvoir was angry with her parents, who she felt had deceived and betrayed her.

In other words, a high achiever can be born first, second, or later. According to Family Theory and Favoritism, a Favored or a Disfavored child can grow up to become a high achiever, but for entirely different reasons. A Favored child can become a high achiever because of her *strong personal connection* with the Prime Love-Giver, a connection that lays the foundation for the child's verbal-intellectual abilities and strong reasoning skills. Building on this positive base, the Favored child may eventually reach great heights of achievement.

On the other hand, a Disfavored child can become a high achiever because of an ongoing *sense of competition* with his siblings. This need to outperform the rival Favored sibling—and thereby win back the Prime Love-Giver's love and attention—is the driving force behind any Disfavored person's efforts to achieve, not only intellectually but also socially and personally. This fact is borne out in the cases of many high-achieving individuals, some of whom candidly expressed their dismay over feeling Disfavored, but many of whom didn't, such as Thomas Merton, Barbra Streisand, Carson McCullers, Grace Kelly, and Phil Donahue.

The Disadvantages of Being Favored

Despite its general appeal, being a Favored child carries its own set of drawbacks. One is that strong ambition and the drive to succeed are not as common among Favored people as they are among Disfavored people. The Favored person, instead of being a high achiever, in fact, frequently isn't aggressive or competitive enough to reach high levels of excellence. The tendency of Favored people to feel content with life often means that they simply feel no need to compete or to progress beyond a certain level of accomplishment.

Contentment in the Favored personality can turn into complacency and eventually prevent personal advancement. This isn't always a bad thing, of course, since personal advancement is not everything in life. However, this kind of unhurried, sometimes self-satisfied attitude can become a stumbling-block in adolescence, when decisions must be made about the future. It can also be a bone of contention between spouses, if one feels that the other ought to be more ambitious or is refusing to deal with the real world aggresively enough.

When Favored people do become successful, they may feel guilty about their achievements. If a Favored person is trying to run a business, for instance, she may not charge enough money for her services and may end up bringing home less pay than she should. Since a Favored child receives most of the Prime Love-Giver's praise and attention, she can end up feeling responsible for overshadowing her Disfavored siblings, both in childhood and in later life. Many Favored children are emotionally mature and capable of appreciating the PLG's reasons for loving their Disfavored sibling less. Yet, like every child, they are deeply familiar with the underground warfare between themselves and their rival, and recognize the ways in which they are actively attracting the parents' love to the detriment of their Disfavored siblings. Caught in this dilemma, a Favored child may perceive the fact that her sibling is Disfavored as her fault, and may come to believe that somehow she doesn't really deserve to advance beyond a certain level. This feeling, in turn, can mean the Favored individual will simply stop trying to achieve, and will settle for less than she is capable of.

Favored individuals tend to be sensitive to other people's feelings in general. Consequently, their shame and sense of guilt are easily aroused. They may take on too much responsibility for events in the family, and because of their compassionate nature, may often give way in an argument. In the harsh reality of life, Favored people are likely to be overpowered by Disfavored individuals, who are often more competitive and more socially manipulative. Someone who is Favored is usually more willing to accommodate or give in to other people and less willing to be persistent or demanding, even when the issue involves protecting his own interests.

Unfortunately, this compassion, coupled with being unaware of other people's deviousness, can lead the Favored person astray. The Favored adolescent is particularly vulnerable in this regard. True, a Favored child is less likely to join a cult or a gang than a Disfavored child, who is searching for the praise and acknowledgment he feels his parents aren't providing. However, a Favored person could join an antisocial group out of good-heartedness, naivety or a sincere interest in the group's ideals. She may not realize that the members intend to try to gain control over her mind and/or material assets. In other words, a Favored person is more likely to take what other people say at face value, while her Disfavored counterpart is instinctively inclined to be more suspicious.

A child who was Favored as he grew up was often protected from life's more painful lessons. As a result, he may be unable to see the difference between a genuine belief and one that has been adopted for unscrupulous ends. And because he has been preferred over his siblings for most of his life, he frequently doesn't appreciate how much love and caring he has always had and how much, therefore, he has to lose.

Another disadvantage of being Favored lies in the treatment the Favored child can receive from her Disfavored siblings. Although they may feel they've done nothing wrong, many Favored siblings have to face the envy, and often the outright hatred, of their less-loved siblings. Treated badly by a jealous Disfavored sibling, the Favored one wonders, "What did I do to deserve this?" Since the Favored person is also sensitive, she can become seriously distressed and lose some of her self-esteem.

Often, however, when shafted by a jealous sister or brother, a Favored sibling doesn't even realize what is going on. Forgiving by nature, and unsuspecting of less-than-honorable motives, the Favored one blindly continues to trust his sibling. After all, he believes, "blood is thicker than water." Consider this example:

> A friend of mine asked her brother's advice on how to start a business. She felt that, since he ran his own business, he was the ideal person to advise her. To her surprise she found that, as well as being discouraging about the possibility of solving certain problems, he sometimes gave her inaccurate information. Moreover, he never forwarded information on relevant conventions that he knew about, and seemed to resist sharing his ideas with her. His excuse was that he didn't have much time to think, but simply had to get on with the job of running the business.
>
> When my friend spoke to me about this situation and I mentioned Favoritism, she clued in immediately. "So that's what it is!" she exclaimed. "I was always so much closer to both my mother and my father than he was. I guess he's been jealous of me all along. I knew there was something wrong, and now that explains it—he doesn't really want me to succeed, does he?"

A jealous Disfavored child who has become used to expressing this anger directly can become openly vicious and abusive toward her Favored sibling. The old Bette Davis movie *What Ever Happened to Baby Jane?* vividly illustrates this kind of extreme sibling-to-sibling hatred. If you recall, it tells the story of a beautiful child film star whose older sister was ignored and neglected by their parents. Later in life, when Baby Jane becomes old and disabled, she goes to live with her sister, who vents her rage by isolating Jane, tormenting her, and subjecting her to various forms of psychological torture.

This is, of course, an extreme scenario! A more common situation is when an older, Disfavored sibling teases a Favored younger child mercilessly. A mother once told me about her daughter, who for years viciously taunted her younger brother about his big ears. As soon as the boy became an adolescent, he announced that he felt he needed surgery to correct his "problem." The mother said she had no idea he had taken his sister's words so much to heart and had felt so badly about his appearance all those years.

The Favored child can also run into difficulties with the Auxiliary Love-Giver, who is another potential competitor for the Prime Love-Giver's love and attention. The ALG may become jealous of the close relationship between the PLG and the Favored child, and may try to usurp the child's position by teasing, belittling, or ignoring him. Again, given the Favored child's gentle nature, he tends to take all expressions of rejection seriously, even though they may appear to be very mild, and thus these experiences can be quite hurtful.

The Favored person's hopeful and sensitive nature places him at great risk for disappointment. This disappointment with events and with the people around him can lead to depression and despair—the feeling that life's not worth living. Many Favored individuals are also burdened by a sense of responsibility about the happiness of others, which can lead to depression. This is clear in the case of Eleanor Roosevelt, whose mother was emotionally unavailable to her, while her father, whom she cherished and by whom she was treasured, was not around. She seems to have worried about the people around her, and sadly, did in fact end up losing them.

Finally, the fact that money is not a priority for the Favored person can be both a strength and a weakness. Generally speaking, Favored people don't feel particularly compelled to accumulate large amounts of money. This ties in with their sense of security, their general confidence about having enough for their needs, and their sense of being satisfied with life. But their trusting nature means they are also more vulnerable to being taken advantage of by people who value the power that money brings and are more financially shrewd.

Overall, the description of the Favored personality shows that there are both advantages and disadvantages to being Favored. Only the circumstances of one's life can show which one will predominate. In general, however, there is little doubt that most people who felt Favored as children are more contented, and will tend to carry this feeling of satisfaction with them into their lives as adults.

11

Handling Your Disfavored and Favored Children

By now, you've probably asked yourself this question: *How much do parents influence their children's personalities by assigning them Favored or Disfavored positions?* The simple answer is a great deal. According to Family Theory and Favoritism, every individual's personality is significantly affected by whether they were Favored or Disfavored as children. Parents contribute to this by harboring preferences for certain personal traits in children, while siblings make their contribution through their efforts to outdo each other. Armed with this knowledge, you can now actively monitor your children's personalities as they develop. When you sense a need to intervene, you can now do it appropriately, and with confidence. Suppose you have a serious problem with your Disfavored child. Here are some explanations and examples of how you should proceed.

The Rescue Operation: Phase One

Intervening in your Disfavored child's life is rather like carrying out a rescue operation. Imagine, if you will, the following scenario: One day, you decide to take a boat ride with your two rival children. Suddenly the boat tips over, and all three of you end up thrashing around in the water in a panic, gasping and yelling. Although both your children are poor swimmers, you know that one child is able to keep afloat, while the other one has a desperate fear of the water. Which child should you rescue first?

Naturally, you follow your impulses and rush to the aid of the child who has the paralyzing fear of water and is screaming the loudest. Under the circumstances, this is obviously the best thing to do, regardless of whether this child is the older or the younger. Meanwhile, you encourage the child who is left behind, telling her to stay calm and tread water until you get back. You leave her in the water temporarily, hoping she'll be able to cope for the few minutes that you need to look after the more helpless one. Even if the child you are rescuing is so terrified that he thrashes about wildly and makes his own rescue difficult, you instinctively persist, knowing his life is at stake.

Step One: Deciding Which Child to Rescue First in a Favoritism Situation

Like the crisis of the capsized boat, a household goes through a great emotional disturbance when the family members are struggling to cope with a difficult Disfavored child. As we discussed in earlier chapters, parents often feel upset and guilty when they recognize their own feelings of Favor and Disfavor toward their children. However, once they accept these feelings and begin coping with their family situation, they have to make a critical decision. Should they turn their attention to the Disfavored child, who appears to be in more distress but who will almost certainly demand a great deal of them, now and in the future? Or should they increase their care for the Favored sibling, who seems to deserve it because he gives them back some gratifyingly positive results for all their hard work?

Faced with a physical threat to their children such as drowning, parents instinctively know what to do first. Yet it's odd that, when they're confronted with a child who is "drowning" on an *emotional* level, parents are baffled. In practice—believe it or not—when a Disfavored child is in obvious distress, *most parents tend to take the side of the better-equipped child, the Favored sibling.* To them, the Favored child is easier to approach, and appears to deserve their affections more because she actively responds to her parents' instructions and doesn't strain their emotional resources. With the Disfavored child, on the other hand, parents may feel they have hit a brick wall. Since he is often more irritable than the Favored child, his parents frequently have given up trying to help.

Most parents, then, despite their best intentions, have a strange tendency to overlook their needy child's debilitating fears and focus instead on the *relative competence* of their capable child. Often, they're so impressed with this child's positive traits and abilities that they become blinded to the Disfavored child, who is truly in trouble and is crying out for their attention in her own way. Beauty, a sunny personality, verbal skills—all those attractive childhood traits that we discussed earlier come into play when they make this choice.

A brief excerpt from the early life of Sylvester Stallone gives a vivid insight into what might happen in a family to bring about the seemingly odd choice that parents make in siding with their Favored child in times of emotional crisis:

> Stallone's mother had difficulty giving birth to him, making a forceps delivery necessary. On taking the baby home, the parents noticed that his left eye drooped, and were told that the forceps had severed one of the major facial nerves, paralyzing one side of his face. Nevertheless, his parents were proud of their son, although he was not to be Favored.
>
> Four years later, they had another son, Frank Jr. This child was perfectly formed and, according to Stallone's biographer, "found the parental favour his elder brother had somehow been denied." Sylvester was a mischievous little boy by now. On one occasion he spray-painted a neighbor's car with red paint, and he had developed the nasty habit of urinating into electrical sockets.
>
> Frank Jr.'s interests were more socially acceptable. He had an aptitude for music, which his parents encouraged by

buying him a saxophone. When they later made the same offer to Sylvester, he rejected it as a careless hand-me-down from his more cherished brother. Later, he took to stealing money from his father's pockets to buy treats for the neighborhood street kids.

It's interesting to note that the family process by which children are divided into Favored and Disfavored positions is *deceptively spontaneous*. It happens without any family member ever meaning to do it. In Sylvester Stallone's case, it seems perfectly natural for his parents to have preferred the son who was interested in music and to have had less love for the child who urinated into power sockets and stole from his father.

Added to the mix, whether parents admit it or not, are the parents' comparisons of their siblings. Looking at their two children, one happily practicing the saxophone and one running outside to spend the money he'd just stolen, Stallone's parents must inevitably have looked at Sylvester and thought, "Why didn't you turn out more like your younger brother?"

Parents faced with a child who acted up as much as Sylvester Stallone might reasonably think that they should punish or discipline him. However, returning to the swimming example, remember that the misbehaving Disfavored child is the less capable one, the one panicking in the water. If you think of it that way, the decision to discipline him now looks totally ridiculous. Punishment would be tantamount to making off with the child who can cope in the water, while yelling at the drowning child, "Why didn't you ever learn to swim?"

Step Two: Rescuing Your Disfavored Child

Rather than making the mistake of rallying to the support of the Favored child, as Stallone's and most parents naturally tend to do, the key to treating a problem with one of your children lies in rescuing the child who is most in need—your Disfavored child. This means that *parents must temporarily concentrate on their Disfavored child's interests.*

Think of it as a form of affirmative action. Parents should show they respect the Disfavored child's nature and are happy to have her as part of the family. Spending time separately with your Disfavored child, getting to know her wants and needs, responding sympathetically to her concerns, are all part of the package, which will be explained further in this chapter.

Without a doubt, turning your attentions to your Disfavored child is the right thing to do to fix the problem. But there are risks involved. Like the boy who couldn't swim, the Disfavored child may kick, scream, and otherwise resist your efforts to rescue him. And you will have to leave the Favored child to fend for herself for a time, while the rest of the family attends to the more immediate emergency situation.

Step Three: Prime and Auxiliary Love-Givers Must Act Together

Before parents take any action, it's a good idea to discuss the problem together and both agree to devote themselves to rescuing their Disfavored child. As every parent knows, it's difficult for just one of them to handle two siblings who are simultaneously demanding attention. This becomes doubly true if one child happens to be in a life-threatening situation, as in our example of the capsized boat. In all aspects of family life, a basic truth is that *neither the PLG nor the ALG alone will be as effective as when they actively work together.* They may have different roles, as we've discussed, but in an emergency situation such as helping a distressed Disfavored child, the PLG and ALG can essentially provide equivalent sources of comfort.

Naturally, the Prime Love-Giver's involvement is essential for any rescue operation. This parent's psychological importance to the children—their unbounded desire for the prime parent's love—makes the PLG indispensable to any recovery process. But the ALG 's cooperation is also important for the child's stability. Because the Disfavored child is emotionally connected not only to the PLG but also to the ALG, this parent can give an enormous—and often decisive—boost to the ultimate success of the rescue. The ALG can significantly speed up the child's process of recovery, and at the same time soothe the general anxiety of the Prime Love-Giver and the rest of the family.

Rescuing a Disfavored child can be made much more difficult for the Prime Love-Giver if the Auxiliary Love-Giver is totally uncooperative. It may be that the ALG is unwilling to help provide the large amount of love that the Disfavored child needs. An uncooperative Auxiliary Love-Giver may also reject the whole idea of Family Theory and Favoritism, and bring in arguments against it that the PLG has to deal with. From the ALG's more cut-and-dried perspective, this parent may feel there's no logical reason to treat the Disfavored child with respect, and may refuse to support either the child or the PLG. Alternatively, the auxiliary parent may simply feel he or she has very little to contribute to the new regime, and use this as an excuse not to become involved. In this case, the Prime Love-Giver should make every effort to persuade the ALG that he or she can help in a positive way.

If the ALG still insists on being uncooperative, the PLG will have to try to work on her or his own. It's far better if *one* parent tries to equalize the situation than if neither parent makes the attempt. Occasionally, the Prime Love-Giver may refuse to participate. In this case, the ALG has little choice but to try to function single-handedly, continuing meanwhile to try to convince the PLG how necessary this remedy is for the whole family's well-being.

Step Four: Accepting the Disfavored Child's Feelings

Once the parents have agreed to work together, it is essential they *accept that the Disfavored child genuinely feels she has been short-changed in terms of the amount of love she is getting at home*. Bear in mind that, whether the problem child is actually Disfavored or not, she definitely *perceives* herself that way. Along with that go the self-centeredness and social immaturity typical of children who believe they are Disfavored. Parents may think these worries over insufficient love are trivial and even groundless, but it's nonetheless important that they acknowledge and respect the fact that the Disfavored child is strongly convinced she is Disfavored.

Opening lines of communication with the Disfavored child is also essential. If parents can help the child share his feelings, they will be better able to understand his point of view. The child will most likely talk about anger and sadness, or remember times in the past when he felt betrayed by family members. As parents listen to these complaints, they must believe that, however self-centered they may sound, their child isn't making up these stories just to get sympathy. He is genuinely hurt, and needs his parents' love, support, and acceptance to feel better. Regardless of their personal reactions, parents must be ready to lend a sympathetic ear and respect the child's concerns. They may be surprised to know that, although the child's behavior might seem totally unreasonable—and at times even bizarre—*his real goal is not to challenge his parents but to win their respect.*

Step Five: Responding to Your Child's Concerns

Once you've listened closely to your Disfavored child's problems and taken them to heart, the best way to respond is by trying to *soothe her distress.* First of all, you need to peel away her defensive outer shell. You can do this by letting her know that you've heard what she's said, you understand and appreciate her feelings, and you want to help. *Often, parents will find that just listening to their child's complaints is enough, and they don't need to take any further drastic action.*

At the same time, parents should honestly be willing to accommodate their child's needs and be ready to show their commitment to this. If you have always refused to have your child's friends over to your house, for instance, because you think they're a bad influence on her, perhaps it's time you invited them. If you've always complained about her messy room, perhaps it's time for you to simply close the door, or offer to help clean up. The best way for parents to prove their good faith is to *act* on some of their Disfavored child's complaints as quickly as possible. If Mary says, "Johnny always hurts me when he hits," don't respond, "But you're eight years old and he's only two." Say, rather, "Then we'll have to teach him to stop doing that to you. Just come and tell me when he does it, and I'll take care of it."

In some cases, parents might consider telling their child that they sincerely regret the fact that they ignored his feelings in the past. *As a last resort*, they might even think about *apologizing* for the genuine mistakes they made because of their own lack of information. However, only do this if you feel the child is old enough to understand and appreciate these comments as the confessions of a sincere and loving parent.

Step Six: Learning What Not to Say

If you do end up apologizing to your Disfavored child, it's important to remember that, even though you may want to share your feelings with her, you should *never, ever admit to having any feelings of Disfavor toward her, now or at any time in the past.* If you had known better, you would certainly have tried to handle things differently. If parents are having trouble coping with the uncomfortable feelings that come with recognizing Favoritism, they should review Chapter 6. Or they should talk to their spouse or friends to relieve the mixture of sadness, guilt, and shame that most parents feel when they first wrestle with Favor and Disfavor. Discussing the problem with other adults can also be a constructive way to share opinions.

Some counseling professionals believe that parents ought to share their deepest feelings with their children. But common sense suggests that this can only lead to trouble. *Almost all frank discussions with the children about actual Favoritism in the family are potentially destructive, both to the Disfavored child and to the parents' relationship with her.* Statements like "I just couldn't help loving your sister more—we're both female and so we have a lot more in common" or "The reason I get along with your brother so well is because he is much better behaved than you" are totally inappropriate. In the same way, comparing one child unfavorably to another—"If only you could be more like your sister"—serves no useful purpose and is certain to lead to arguments and hurt feelings on every side. This kind of irresponsible discussion with children can also result in a communication deadlock with the Disfavored child and jeopardize any hope of future progress, since it confirms the child's lurking suspicions about being second best. And as far as the child is concerned, this is, if you recall, almost the same as total rejection.

Parents should keep in mind that, according to Family Theory and Favoritism, there never really was, and never will be, a perfect solution to the problem of Favoritism. The only way to end your children's rivalry over the PLG's love would be to eliminate one of the children—which is hardly realistic! They should accept the fact that their children will never fully come to terms with this dilemma, until perhaps they themselves become parents one day.

On the other hand, parents should not hesitate to admit to their Disfavored child that *they didn't realize how seriously unhappy he had been.* They can certainly say they weren't aware of their child's suffering in the past, and they didn't know that he saw himself as second best. They might say something like, "We didn't realize you felt so badly, and we're truly sorry that we didn't do anything about it earlier."

During their conversations with the Disfavored child, parents should try to focus on *their child's* feelings of betrayal, and not get sidetracked into other issues, such as their own pain, the damage that has been done to the family, or how hard they've tried to cope in the past. *The pressing issue is the child's unhappiness, not the parents' or the other children's distress.*

Finally, if cooling the Disfavored child's anger is all that's needed to keep the peace for a while, parents would do well to maintain this truce for as long as possible while they try to build on the positive aspects of their relationship with the child. When parents suddenly stop criticizing and begin to show genuine affection and concern toward the Disfavored child instead, they often find that *she temporarily becomes disarmed.* In other words, by suddenly changing course and treating the child with respect, they will have taken the wind out of her sails, and she may be temporarily stunned into behaving better.

The Rescue Operation: Phase Two

As you now know, all children are irresistibly attracted to the love that their parents provide, and it is each child's hope and dream to be the single ally of the Prime Love-Giving parent. Despite children's reluctance to tell adults about this dream, we can see proof of it in two ways: the deep bitterness that children demonstrate when they realize they are not Favored, and the fact that they are eternally attracted to their parents' love, even if it suddenly becomes available for no clear reason. Because of this need, parents can sometimes bring about a temporary truce just by following the steps of Phase One, in which they focus their love on their Disfavored child.

However, as many parents soon learn, all their efforts to be caring and generous might still not be enough to discourage the Disfavored child's undesirable behavior. There may seem to be no end to his problems and demands. Many Disfavored children stubbornly resist their parents' loving approaches from the very beginning, while others only improve their behavior temporarily. As the parents give in more and more in their attempt to show they truly love their child, the child may simply respond by *demanding more*. Meanwhile, he remains basically dissatisfied. In fact, in most cases, parents who turn their love and attention to a Disfavored child, even if this love really comes from their hearts, haven't yet won the battle to significantly change their Disfavored child's attitude.

The reason for this is simple. It goes back to one of the central issues I've discussed throughout this book—the instinct-driven, rather than logic-driven, thinking of a child. In her self-centered mind the Disfavored child continues to compare herself with the Favored one. It's not usually discussed openly, but the issue of *comparison* returns to haunt us, and to poison the Disfavored child's thoughts. Her immature mind continues to ask not only "Do my parents love me?" but "Do my parents love me *the most*?" Despite her parents' increased love and attention, she still wonders, "Can I actually replace my sibling in my parents' hearts?"

For it is the *quality* of this precious love between the PLG and the Favored sibling that the Disfavored child envies. Her secret, desperate wish is to *replace* the Favored one. The most cherished desire of every Disfavored child is to be loved not only as much as but *more than* the Favored child, and to occupy the coveted spot that the Favored child now holds with the Prime Love-Giver.

Ultimately, just as comparison with the Favored sibling opens the door to the Disfavored child's bad behavior, *comparison is the only key that can heal him*. Comparing him with his rival brother or sister is still the critical factor that can "turn off" his negative feelings, and "turn on" his positive feelings toward the family and the outside world. This means that, however much parents may focus on their Disfavored child, *his behavior may not improve much unless the issue of rivalry with his proximate sibling is settled.*

Parents thus have to try to balance the odds by doing their best to indulge the Disfavored child's fantasy and attempt to love her in the same way as they love the Favored child. This involves trying to create the same type of closeness, attachment and unspoken mutual love that currently exists only between the Prime Love-Giver and the Favored sibling.

Step One: Convincing Yourself that Your Disfavored Child Is As Lovable As Your Favored Child

As with Phase One, the first step in Phase Two of rescuing your child is to work on *your own* feelings. Parents must convince themselves that their Disfavored child's positive traits are as worthy of their love as those of their Favored one.

Some parents might think this task of equalizing their feelings about their two children, who may be polar opposites, utterly impossible. It's not, but it is extremely difficult. In fact, *providing absolutely equal affection* is one of the greatest obstacles that any parent, whether prime or auxiliary, may have to overcome.

Many parents feel that summoning up the same amount of affection for each child is too artificial, especially considering their bad relationship with their Disfavored child and the child's ongoing negative behavior. In their heart of hearts, they find it hard to believe that this kind of equal love can realistically be achieved. The anguished parent protests, "Can I *really* love both children equally? Or would I just be lying to myself—and to my Disfavored child—if I *pretended* to love her as much as the Favored one?" This is a legitimate question. But the fact remains that, if parents truly want to help their Disfavored child, they must try as best they can to communicate a great deal of affection toward the Disfavored child, even though it may feel strange at the beginning, and be as genuine as possible in doing it.

It's crucial how much *faith* parents have in their Disfavored child's ability to please them in the same ways as their Favored child. Since their standards for the Disfavored child are likely to be the same as those they apply to the Favored one, what are the Disfavored child's real prospects for being more closely allied with her parents? Parents will have to ask themselves whether their standards can be stretched to include the Disfavored child's abilities and her limitations, and begin to work toward changing these standards to include her.

In some extreme cases, parents may have to struggle with yet another serious question: *How far will they go in terms of sacrificing their personal and social needs for the sake of repairing the relationship with their Disfavored child?* How much are they willing to give up for the sake of attaining a truce? Should they give up their own comforts and peace of mind for the sake of a truce? The parent might ask: "Is peace a realistic possibility? How far am I willing to go to achieve it? Is it worth jeopardizing my lifestyle and my family's lifestyle in order to attain it? What effect will it have on the rest of the family, including the other children?"

Some parents may need to convince themselves that the whole process of reclaiming their Disfavored child is worthwhile. To motivate themselves, they can begin by making an inventory of the Disfavored child's positive qualities. If a child is a member of a street gang, for example, parents might think, "Although we disapprove of what our son is doing, his joining a gang shows that he's a loyal person; he is physically strong and is willing to help others in the gang who are less able; he has the courage of his convictions; he is our only son," and so on.

On the other hand, they might want to encourage their own concern for the child by thinking about his helplessness. They might take pity on the child and contemplate the bleak future he'll face if he doesn't change. They might think about their own suffering, as well as the social disgrace they have endured because of this child, and then consider the joy that would come out of a reconciliation. They might even think about their own future needs, and their possible dependence on the child as they grow older.

Step Two: Discounting Heredity and Other Myths

Parents should try to dismiss heredity and other myths that might mislead them about what to expect from their child. As I discussed early in this book, all myths about the source of their child's bad behavior being simply bad genes, bad cultural values (television, movies, advertising, and so on), bad peer influences and the like should be ignored. These myths not only deceive parents but offer them no real hope. They merely allow them to transfer the blame to issues that they can't change. It's far better to devote your energy to changing what is possible and what you can see. Besides, based on Family Theory and Favoritism, every parent can rely on the fact that if it weren't for this particular Disfavored child, there would most probably have been another with equally undesirable behavior whom they would have had to deal with.

Step Three: Building the Disfavored Child's Self-Esteem

In order for the Disfavored child to become more receptive to your new attitude, one of your main responsibilities is to *build up her self-esteem*. One good way to do this is to find activities that your Disfavored child can perform *as well as, if not better than, your Favored one*. This will serve a dual purpose: it will help convince you that your Disfavored child has good qualities, while at the same time developing her self-confidence.

Here, your determination and creativity must come into play. Can you think of an area in which your Disfavored child can compete successfully with the rival sibling and gain praise for her excellent performance? Are there any areas in which your Disfavored child actually performs better than her rival sibling? Remember, however, to stay clear of any spoken comparisons, either with siblings or with outsiders, since this can greatly undermine a child's self-esteem.

Physical demonstrations of love—hugs, kisses, pats—which are always nourishing to a child's self-esteem, should be kept up or revived with the Disfavored child. Particularly if the child is young, physical contact is an important way of communicating affection. If the child or the parents happen to dislike touching or find it inappropriate, then eye contact and expressing a verbal interest in how he's getting on are valid alternatives.

Step Four: Persisting in Your Rescue

A woman once told me about a problem situation with her Disfavored daughter. I explained a bit about Family Theory and Favoritism, and suggested some strategies that she could apply to help change her daughter's attitude. She called me some time later to tell me she'd followed my instructions with great success.

A year later she called again to announce that the same behavioral problems were slowly resurfacing. When I asked her whether she was still using the same techniques of encouragement and equalization that I had recommended, she replied, "Oh no! You don't expect me to keep *that* up all the time!"

Persistence is an important part of any parent's efforts to change a Disfavored child's behavior. Being kind to a Disfavored child might be a strain at times, and a parent might question the need for it. But in order to maintain your Disfavored child's good behavior, *it is necessary that you carrying on reassuring and praising her.* Part of being able to do this involves convincing yourself that you do indeed love this child as much as you love the Favored sibling. At the same time, you also have to convince the child that this is true. Eventually, as new behavior patterns become established in the family, tempers will cool, rivalry will decrease, and there will be less need for parents to pay such constant attention to their child.

Step Five: Dealing with Your *Favored* Child

As parents set about rescuing their Disfavored child, they should also be carefully monitoring their Favored child's reaction to these changes. It is up to parents to help this child adjust to the family's new social structure as well. Even though the Favored child may well be more secure than the Disfavored one, he still needs his parents' love and attention. To this end, they must try hard to maintain the deep emotional connection they have always enjoyed with him, since this relationship will inevitably be put to the test by the change in the family's dynamics.

As a normal, competitive sibling himself, the Favored child has, of course, become used to holding a privileged position in the family, and she will be highly sensitive to losing any social ground. With the changes in the way the family behaves together, the Favored sibling may suddenly become resentful and angry, or inexplicably sullen and silent. She may become more vocal and aggressive—yelling at her parents, for instance, or picking fights with her siblings. Or she may lose some of her self-esteem and wonder, "What did I do wrong?"

Again, parents must respond with sensitivity. To go back to the example of the capsized boat, they usually have an *unspoken* confidence in their Favored child's ability to pull through this ordeal, as she has always done in the past. But in a rescue situation, where more love is suddenly being directed toward the Disfavored child, it is sometimes necessary for parents to increase their *demonstrations* of confidence in the Favored sibling as well, either verbally, through reassuring words, or physically, with extra hugs or some special time set aside to spend with this child alone.

Parents should bear in mind that *the Favored child has a vested interest in maintaining her image of superiority in the family.* When parents try to give both children equal attention, the Favored child will try desperately to hang on to her supremacy. She might do this by putting down the Disfavored sibling, showing off, or trying to manipulate situations so that adults see her in a more positive light than the Disfavored child.

Keep an especially keen lookout for this kind of behavior. As we've noted before, children have subtle ways of expressing their natural animosities, and adults often fail to notice this kind of rivalry altogether or, if they do, don't take it seriously. Most adults don't realize that children's verbal assaults on each other can be extremely destructive. For this reason, parents must remain sharply attuned to any teasing or belittling that the Favored child inflicts on the Disfavored one, either as a habit from the past or as a new tactic since the establishment of the family's new social order. This type of psychological warfare is aimed at destroying the opposition from within, and children are acutely sensitive to these provocations. It is just this kind of needling that makes them respond to each other with massive amounts of rage and hurt.

If the Favored child tries to control the Disfavored one by insulting him, embarrassing him, or subjecting him to other forms of verbal abuse, parents must step in and strictly forbid this kind of behavior. They should clearly show that, although they still love the Favored child very dearly, such behavior is not acceptable. In fact, even though parents may understand exactly why their Favored child is behaving this way, and may sympathize with her efforts to stop the family arrangement from changing, they should nonetheless not hesitate to discipline the Favored child if such attacks continue. If parents persist with their new attitude toward both Disfavored and Favored children, they will find that over time the Favored child will settle down and the relationship between the two rivals will gradually improve.

Another important aspect of dealing with your Favored child is to remember *never to discuss the Disfavored child, or your new family strategy, with the Favored one.* Regardless of how mature the Favored child may seem, parents should remember that *all* children are essentially self-centered and thus want to acquire social supremacy in the family. Despite her apparent ability to identify with adults' concerns, the Favored child is still a child, and this means that discussing the new approach with her is completely inappropriate. In some cases, it might even be counterproductive, in that it could further fuel the fires of rivalry.

Finally, with time, the parents' change in attitude should have a positive effect not only on the Disfavored child but on the Favored child as well. People with a Favored personality are typically kind, generous, and forgiving. They are also often easygoing, and because of this, tend to follow rather than lead. Under the new social order in the family, in which the rival Disfavored sibling is treated as equally exemplary and praiseworthy, the Favored child is likely to adopt some new competitive behaviors of her own, which will help her in life. In this way, the rebalancing of parental attitudes is likely to be a positive step for the entire family, even though the short run may seem a little gruelling at times.

What Eventually Happens: The Reversal Effect and Leverage

If most of the above conditions are put into effect, parents can expect to see a gradual *reversal effect* in their children. The reversal effect happens when the Favored and Disfavored children begin to trade places. Surprising as it may seem, if parents reverse their attitudes, *the Disfavored child will gradually begin to take on some of the softer characteristics of the Favored personality*, while the Favored child will become a little more angry, depressed, and anxious.

In response to his parents' more sympathetic attitude, the Disfavored child slowly moves toward being able to fulfill more of his parents demands. With time, a lot of the anger, sadness, and anxiety expressed through his behavior diminishes. He becomes a little more mature, communicates better, and is gradually able to build up trust in others. He will also have greater respect for adults and their values, and will be less likely to oppose them at every turn. In some cases, this change is gradual, occurring over a period of years, but in others, it can be a very dramatic turnaround that takes place in a matter of days or weeks.

At the same time, parents may see a partial reversal effect in their Favored child as well. This means that he may take on Disfavored characteristics. He might show more anger and aggression, be more obviously unhappy with the status quo, and begin to challenge his parents' values and demands. However, because of the Favored strengths that have already been established in his personality, it's not too difficult in most cases for parents to keep this child emotionally on track.

A dramatic reversal effect is often most evident in small children. To the shock and amazement of many parents, their "angel" and their "devil" may suddenly change places! The previously Disfavored child becomes sweet and compliant, while the Favored one takes on the aggression, sadness, or anxiety typical of a Disfavored child. While these changes may be surprising or disturbing, they also demonstrate how much power parents have to influence their children's behavior. This transformation clearly illustrates how children depend so wholeheartedly on their parents' attitudes for the formation of their personalities, and is living proof of Family Theory and Favoritism.

Once parents have successfully changed their attitudes toward their Disfavored child, they can also expect to acquire a certain amount of *leverage* or influence over him. *Leverage is a result of the empathy that develops between parents and their children, once the child begins to believe that her parents really love and respect her as an individual.* The idea that they care for the Disfavored child as much as they do for the Favored sibling has a softening effect on the child's feelings, and therefore on her behavior. Although she may still hang on to some of the negative behavior patterns that led to the problem in the first place, the parents now hold some valuable leverage, rooted in loving feelings, that can help them advise, encourage, and teach their Disfavored child to behave in more positive ways.

This harks back to the discussion about Behavioral Theory, in which I emphasized that, in the case of human beings, a reward-and-punishment system won't work *unless the individual wants to change.* Otherwise, no amount of reward or punishment is effective. Leverage—which becomes possible through the new-found positive relationship with the child—provides this key. Unlocking the door to the child's *desire* to cooperate paves the way for a new beginning.

Although the relationship with the Disfavored child may never be perfect, it will certainly have reached the point where parents can ask for, and expect, more concessions from the child than they ever could before. Once this is established, parents and children will have a new empathy and understanding on which they can build their relationship.

Finally, even if there seems to be very little immediate disruption in the household, it is still important to search out feelings of Disfavor among children, and work toward resolving them. The first great advantage is that relationships between parents and children, as well as between rival siblings, can be smoothed out. In addition, the quality of life for the Disfavored child will be immeasurably improved. Greatly decreased, on the other hand, will be the child's tension associated with poor self-image, and that comes from feeling second best. Everyone's energy can then be focused in more positive directions. Don't forget, too, that parents are so often taken by surprise by their children's actions: Why did my child suddenly join a cult? Why did he go on drugs? Why did she kill herself? Short of perfection, which is unrealistic, using the principles of Family Theory and Favoritism, the whole family will have more peace of mind and more love to share with one another.

12

Applying Family Theory and Favoritism to Other Family Situations

Family Theory and Favoritism doesn't just apply to parents who are having problems dealing with their children. It also provides an overall method of personality analysis that holds true for everyone, including adults, since we all have a family of origin. Using Family Theory and Favoritism as a tool, you can solve a variety of individual and family problems. What follows are several examples of circumstances in which you could use this new framework.

Family Planning

By providing a scheme for analyzing family dynamics, Family Theory and Favoritism adds a certain measure of *predictability* to family life. In fact, with this new approach you can, to a certain extent, anticipate the various roles in the family before they actually develop. Naturally, at the beginning of a marriage, talk about being either the Prime or Auxiliary Love-Giver is basically speculation. It is only after the first baby arrives that parents' roles can be decided, since this choice depends on the spontaneous reactions of each parent to their first child.

However, family analysis can begin as soon as the first child is born, and continue as more children are added. In this way, parents can get a head start on dealing with feelings of Favor and Disfavor as they come up.

Parents-to-be may want to think about what Family Theory and Favoritism says about the only child, as well as about two-, three-, and four-sibling families. If they plan to have only one child, they may want to go over the virtues and perils of the single-child family that are outlined in a section toward the end of this chapter. If a couple plans for a small to medium-sized family, they could aim to *minimize the number of Disfavored children*. As I mentioned earlier, two- and four-sibling families have a strong tendency to fall into a 50-50 Favored-Disfavored split among the children. In a three-sibling family, however, there can be a greater proportion of Favored children. The combinations F D F and D F F, for instance, contain only one Disfavored sibling out of three, which means there will be only one child who is likely to require extra attention.

If parents realize that their third child is Favored, they might think twice about having a fourth, since the fourth child who follows a Favored third one will almost certainly be Disfavored. On the other hand, if the existing combination is D F D, with the third child Disfavored, a fourth child will probably create a new cluster with the youngest one. Out of this cluster, one of the two younger siblings will eventually emerge as Favored, most likely the baby.

Child Custody

In cases of separation and divorce, parents' anger toward each other often interferes with their judgment of what is best for their children. An Auxiliary Love-Giver who has been relatively detached from the children, for instance, might nonetheless demand custody to get back at the spouse. A large part of this parent's anger usually stems from having felt left out of the Circle of Love throughout the time the family was together. Thus, an ALG might ask for custody to force at least a partial inclusion in the family fold.

A variation on the same theme might involve a mother who has always stayed at home but is in fact the Auxiliary rather than the Prime Love-Giver. She may feel entitled to keep the children simply because she has been used to spending a great deal of time with them. Yet if their father is the PLG, the children will suffer if they don't spend a good deal of time with him.

The distinction between the Prime and Auxiliary Love-Giver, made on the basis of their emotional importance to their children, becomes highly significant in resolving problems of child custody. Ideally, children should have their Prime Love-Giver as their principal guardian, since the PLG is the parent to whom they are more emotionally attached, regardless of this parent's gender. This arrangement is psychologically healthiest for all concerned. Even if the PLG can't arrange to have the children live in her or his house, it is still important for this parent to have as much access to them as possible.

As you saw earlier, despite the fact that most people traditionally think of women as Prime Love-Givers, men seem to assume this role in about half of all families. In fairness to everyone, then, the question "Who is the Prime Love-Giver?" should be answered as objectively as possible before any decisions about child custody are made. It might be helpful to talk to a variety of interested parties, including members of the extended family and friends, as well as the children themselves.

When deciding who should be a child's principal guardian, it's important to remember that a Prime Love-Giver and a primary caregiver are not necessarily the same. Society tends to see the primary caregiver as the parent *who spends more time attending to the child's physical needs*, and judges often use this as a guide when they make decisions about custody. On the other hand, the Prime Love-Giver is the parent *who gives the child the most emotional warmth*. It's a distinction that can be difficult to make at times, but it is well worth keeping in mind in custody cases.

In cases where the Prime Love-Giver loses custody or the right to significant access, you can expect to see the children become confused and unhappy. As you now know, *separation from the PLG can take a significant emotional toll on a family*. With society's current bias in favor of mothers, the mistake of awarding children to the less emotionally nourishing parent is most likely to occur in cases where the father is the Prime Love-Giver but is unrecognized as holding this position in the family.

Joint custody, which may seem to be the fairest solution to the problem of child custody, also has enormous pitfalls. While it may satisfy the possessive impulses of two squabbling adults, joint custody can be compared to the solution proposed by King Solomon, who threatened to cut the baby in half in order to resolve an argument over who the child's mother was. The problem with joint custody is that it assumes both partners have equal emotional significance to the children, which Family Theory has shown to be untrue. Joint custody may be appropriate in some cases, such as when the Prime Love-Giver can't be as available to the children as the Auxiliary Love-Giver, but if the Prime Love-Giver is able and willing, it is usually better all round if this parent becomes the principal custodian.

As most separated or divorced parents realize, the battle for custody is almost always complex and laden with emotion for everyone concerned. This is especially true with a Disfavored child, who isn't easy to handle at the best of times. Since divorce adds to children's insecurity, a Disfavored child, who is more insecure from the start, is more likely to suffer from its effects. The following story is a good example of the possible side-effects of divorce on a Disfavored child.

> Katherine was a Disfavored child who was having problems with her Prime Love-Giver—in this case, her mother. Their constant arguments finally resulted in Katherine deciding to try living with her ALG father instead, while her Favored brother, Robert, stayed in the mother's home.
>
> Soon after Katherine moved in with her father, however, she was sadly disappointed. Leaving her Prime Love-Giving mother and Robert alone together only added to Katherine's agony. Even though Katherine herself had decided to make the change, she felt even more rejected and

abandoned than she had when she was living with her mother and brother, and her decision simply felt like another failure.

Ideally, it would have been better for Katherine to have stayed with Robert and her Prime Love-Giving mother, in the hope of resolving her difficulties. Even though her parents were divorced, it would have been helpful if they had recognized that Katherine was feeling Disfavored and had collaborated to try to help her feel more secure *in her mother's home*, rather than allowing her to follow her impulses and leave. Emotionally, it would have been healthier for her mother, too, since she also ended up feeling she had failed her daughter.

In some sad cases, the relationship between a PLG and a Disfavored child truly goes sour and becomes distinctly harmful to one of them. This can happen if the PLG blatantly discriminates against the Disfavored child, or if the child is totally out of control when she is with the Prime Love-Giver. In these instances, the Disfavored child might actually benefit from the chance to escape to a neutral environment. If the ALG or any other benevolent adult could provide a more loving environment than the PLG's home, this arrangement might well work out to everyone's satisfaction.

Tormenting the Youngest Child

A common problem with middle children often happens in a three-sibling family when a very frustrated middle child systematically harasses the youngest one. This gives the impression that there is a fierce rivalry between these two siblings, but on further examination, it turns out that the strongest source of rivalry is, in fact, between the middle child and the older one.

Most often in this situation, the first child is Favored and the middle one is Disfavored (as in the combinations F D F or F D D). An example is the case of ten-year-old Peter, a middle child who hated his Disfavored status but couldn't confront his older, Favored brother,

Jack, who, at fifteen, was just too physically and verbally powerful for Peter to challenge. In other instances, the middle child feels unable to take on the older Favored sibling because the connection between this sibling and the Prime Love-Giver is very strong, and the middle child feels he just can't break this tight connection.

Since Peter was unable to get angry at Jack, he looked for an alternate outlet for his pent-up rage. The most convenient was his younger sister, Janet, who, because she was only six, was both physically and verbally less capable of protecting herself.

Peter used every form of insult and injury imaginable toward little Janet, drawing on a mixed bag of obvious methods—name-calling or hitting—and others that were barely noticed by his parents, such as whispered insults, systematic belittling, pinching, and so on. Part of Peter knew just how unfair his actions were, and sometimes he felt guilty about being so mean. Yet at the same time, he was incredibly frustrated by Jack's Favored position and got an immense sense of power and pleasure from being ruthless toward his little sister.

While this scenario may not look particularly harmful at first, it can be very serious for the youngest child if the middle one progresses to outright viciousness and cruelty. Her brother told her she was stupid so many times that eventually Janet began to believe it, and she became distressed to the point that she found most intellectual challenges too intimidating. As Janet's self-esteem dwindled, she saw fewer and fewer friends, and sank to the bottom of her class. Certainly, compared to her two older brothers, she didn't seem to be very sharp-witted.

Peter and Janet's parents gradually gave up trying to resolve this strife, tragically ignoring the pattern of emotional battery that Peter was inflicting on his sister. Worst of all, they became convinced that Janet was in fact incompetent, and began to deal with her as if she were far less intelligent than her brothers. Unfortunately, this is a very common reaction. The parents simply resign themselves to this state of affair, thinking, "I guess our youngest daughter just isn't as bright as the rest of the family. She probably takes after Aunt Marge, who had to leave school early because she got pregnant (or Uncle Tom who never amounted to anything)."

Applying Favoritism to this problem, parents could identify the *actual* source of the middle child's agitation. They could pinpoint the real center of rivalry: between the first, Favored child (in our example, Jack) and the second, Disfavored child (Peter). Once parents had located the true center of the conflict—in the relationship between the first two siblings—they could begin, as we discussed in the previous chapter, to balance their attitudes and feelings toward their first two children. In particular, the Prime Love-Giver would have to loosen the ties with the first child in order to make more room for the middle one. The frustrated middle child could then participate more successfully in the Circle of Love with the PLG, thereby reducing his anxieties. Most importantly, it would *release the emotional pressure on the youngest child* and give her some space to regain her self-assurance.

To help this process along, the parents could also intervene verbally on the youngest child's behalf if they sensed that she was in need of immediate protection, as Janet was. Knowing that belittling can damage anyone's self-esteem, they could step in whenever they overheard the middle child being unkind to the youngest. If the youngest child began to rely too heavily on her parents' protection, they could always gently encourage her to defend herself. Later on, when they felt she could do this effectively, they could gradually decrease their interventions.

Such tactics have to be used with care, however. If a special alliance starts to develop between the youngest sibling and the PLG *without empowering the Disfavored middle child at the same time*, this may only irritate him further. As a result, he may become even more aggressive or be driven away from the family altogether.

Sibling Babysitting

Most people assume that you can safely leave a younger sibling in the care of an older one. The myth that siblings should be the best of friends, along with the fact that such an arrangement is frequently very convenient for the parents, means that many parents automatically rely on sibling babysitting.

However, your new knowledge, not only about children's fundamental selfishness but also about the way they perceive each other as rivals, should alert you to the potential for friction in this situation. Entrusting children to one another's care provides the ideal opportunity to express deep-seated animosities, creating situations in which both older and younger siblings can suffer. An older child might take advantage of her position of authority, for instance, by bossing the younger ones around or otherwise undermining them. On the other hand, younger children might take advantage of the tension they sense in an older child when she is placed in a position of responsibility. They might gang up on her, talk back, break rules, or otherwise torment the older sibling who has been left in charge.

Here is a description of how siblings really feel toward each other, drawn from the experiences of one man:

> Abbie Hoffman was a well-known social activist in the sixties. His brother Jack, three years younger, describes him as a loving and protective older brother but also one who always let him know who was boss. As early as Jack could remember, every night Abbie would eject him from their shared bed with a solid kick. One day, as they were wrestling together, Abbie kicked his brother in the groin. Immediately afterward, though, as a kind of silent apology, he took Jack upstairs and spent an hour teaching him how to play chess.
>
> Jack concludes that there's an exclusive friendship among brothers that is "colder hearted" than a parent's love, yet simpler and more direct. After pondering on this strange love-hate relationship, Jack frankly says that, without any animosity intended toward his late brother, he believes that "[i]t's almost impossible for an older brother to resist being a bully [to a younger one]."

In dealing with family babysitting, as with any other sibling interactions, it's important for parents to listen to the reports of both the younger and the older children, especially after they've been left to fend for themselves for a while. Allowing them to recount their experiences not only serves to relieve their emotional stress, but also helps keep the lines of communication open with their parents, who can then figure out what is *really* going on.

At the worst, sibling babysitting—like babysitting by anyone else—can lead to physical or sexual abuse. This, of course, is all the more reason for parents to talk to their children, keep involved with their lives, and closely monitor babysitting situations.

High Achievement

A common hidden expression of sibling rivalry is the tendency of some children, both Favored and Disfavored, to become high achievers in school. Instead of adopting direct expressions of rivalry, such as fighting, some Disfavored children will channel their powerful competitive drives into intellectual pursuits and gear themselves toward outdoing their rival siblings academically.

For the Disfavored child, academic excellence can become an important way of gaining the respect and praise of adults. Scholastic achievement frequently goes along with social sensitivity and maturity—traits that appeal to adults. The child seems to have both the verbal-intellectual qualities and the social appeal that make him likable. He does and says the right things at the right time, behaves in a way that pleases adults, and is sensitive to what's important to them. It's no wonder that this kind of child is often chosen as the teacher's pet in school.

Looking at this behavior, it might initially seem that the achieving Disfavored child is switching from his original status to a Favored position. However, *the Disfavored personality established during early childhood tends to remain largely the same*, although the intellectually competitive Disfavored child often appears more attractive to adults than other

Disfavored children. While the child may be performing marvelously according to social standards, his competitive anxiety stays well hidden. In fact, from a social point of view, academic competition, as well as any other forms of competition such as sports, music, social activities, etc., are very positive ways for children to channel their competitive energies. The example of Nancy Greene is a good one:

> Nancy Greene, Canadian winner of an Olympic gold medal for skiing in 1968, probably represents the epitome of our idea of healthy competition. In her autobiography, Nancy is acutely aware of having developed an intense rivalry with her sister Elizabeth, two years older, who was a proficient skier. Nancy admits that she probably delayed her own entry into competitive skiing because at the beginning she didn't dare challenge her sister.
>
> She shows admirable honesty and insight into her motivations for achievement. Although she has a younger sister, Judy, who posed a challenge to her as well, Nancy candidly declares that once she caught the bug for racing, her first and foremost ambition was to beat her older sister, Liz.

From a parent's point of view, it's wonderful if children channel their sibling rivalry into academic, sports-related, or other accepted competitive pursuits. It can lead to pride, peace of mind, and an end to hostilities on the home front. Experience shows that *such socially acceptable ways of competing are often found in homes where both the PLG and ALG are active and significant contributors to raising the children.* Having been well parented, all the children, whether Favored or Disfavored, are inclined to develop a high level of skill in many areas, whether verbal, physical, social, or academic.

Inheritance

When parents die, problems around Favoritism that had their roots in the family of origin return to haunt the grown-up children.

Undercurrents of resentment that have festered for decades suddenly resurface once the parents are gone. Adult siblings may now feel freer to express deep-rooted feelings of jealousy, and many Disfavored adults try to grab and hoard their parents' possessions, a telling sign that they felt they were treated with less love and respect than the other children. It's as if the money or property were "owed" to the Disfavored children to compensate for the love they missed during their parents' lifetime.

In arguments involving inheritance, some people make claims that are clearly unreasonable. Disfavored siblings, with their greater competitiveness and interest in money, are likely to fight harder for their parents' material goods than their Favored counterparts. They usually approach the matter of dividing the estate with a more businesslike attitude, while the Favored siblings tend to get so caught up in their sorrow over the loss of their parents that they forget to be concerned about mundane issues like money. The Favored adult's distress when a parent dies also leaves her more vulnerable to the guile of the Disfavored sibling, who is typically more shrewd.

When the PLG Is Unrecognized

One of the most common family problems is the situation where the Prime Love-Giver is insufficiently recognized within a family. The PLG performs her or his important emotional role as the main provider of love to the family, but is actively undermined by an aggressive Auxiliary Love-Giver, who may be pushy, domineering, critical, or even outright violent toward the Prime Love-Giver.

The ALG may even try to displace this parent to some degree, so that, to the uninformed observer, the PLG might look rather passive and less involved in the family's functioning than the ALG, who appears to be carrying most of the load. Often there are complaints from the ALG about how much work she or he is doing to keep the family going.

Yet the truth is that the prime parent is being overshadowed by the aggressive auxiliary parent. For the children, this distinction between the parents is—and always will be—crystal clear. As we have said, as a result of their sharply attuned social instincts, children recognize Prime and Auxiliary Love-Giving functions from the very first stages of family life. They make no mistake.

In the case of an interfering ALG, the Prime Love-Giver notes not only the ALG's domination but also possibly her or his own inability to handle the Disfavored child's negative behavior—a common problem for many PLGs, given their soft-heartedness. As a result, the PLG becomes convinced that she or he is an ineffective parent, and backs off from providing the family's main emotional nurturing. The family tension mounts when the PLG, who is being morally battered by the ALG, then abdicates from dealing with the Disfavored child.

As the relationship between the PLG and the Disfavored child deteriorates, the ALG increasingly deals with the Disfavored child's behavior. And while it may be true that the ALG is a skilled disciplinarian, she or he is also prone to treating the Disfavored child quite harshly and with little sympathy. Meanwhile, the PLG's connection with the Favored child remains strong, so the Disfavored child continues to be hurt and angry.

A PLG can be underrated when either the mother or the father is the prime parent. The father could be the Prime Love-Giver and the mother an anxious, controlling ALG who constantly undermines and criticizes him. In fact, this particular configuration, in which the underrated PLG is the father, tends to be reinforced by the secondary status our society routinely assigns to fathers when it comes to raising children. In this kind of family, nobody ever seems to suspect how important the father's input really is, usually including the father himself. In a crisis with a Disfavored child, the social bias against him as the PLG prompts him either to withdraw from family interaction, and give up trying to deal with the Disfavored child, or to resort to tough disciplinary measures as an attempt to fix the problem.

The same situation can occur when the mother is the Prime Love-Giver and *her* status is systematically undermined by an overaggressive husband. If a wife is emotionally or physically battered by her mate, the abuse takes away her power and prevents her from dealing effectively with the children. In time, she may begin to lose confidence in her ability to be an effective parent and stop trying to cope with problem behavior. Again, as with the PLG father, this especially interferes in her dealings with her Disfavored child, as she may give up trying to deal with the child and delegate this responsibility to her stricter, ALG spouse.

A similar scenario can occur when an Auxiliary Love-Giver tries, with the best of intentions, to relieve the PLG, but matters just escalate. Consider the example of Eric, a Disfavored son who craved his mother's attention, since she was the PLG, but tried to get it by behaving provocatively toward her. Not realizing how important the relationship was between his son and the mother, even though it appeared troubled on the surface, Eric's ALG father tried to intervene as the family disciplinarian. Punishment sometimes worked to force Eric into line temporarily, but at other times, his father's discipline not only seemed to accomplish little but made matters worse. In fact, severe discipline can plunge a Disfavored child into depression, and this was eventually what happened to Eric. He felt overpowered and alienated from the family, and ended up hating his father and arguing with him constantly.

By trying to discipline Eric, his parents were focusing on the wrong area. A bitter conflict developed between the ALG father and Eric, the Disfavored child, but in fact it was *the mother's love and attention* that was the key. This is likely to happen whenever the rift between the PLG and the Disfavored child becomes too great and the job of dealing with the child's misbehavior is delegated to the ALG.

Applying Favoritism in order to understand the *child* and make an accurate analysis of a situation is essential to resolving the conflicts created when a Prime Love-Giver is unacknowledged or undermined. If the Auxiliary Love-Giver, whether the father or the mother, is undercutting the Prime Love-Giver's role, she or he should stop doing so and instead assume the secondary parenting role. The ALG can even help the PLG develop a better and closer relationship with the Disfavored child, which will benefit the child and, in the end, enhance the emotional health of the entire family.

In the last example, Eric's father would be advised to tone down the discipline and allow Eric's mother to try to solve the problem with their misbehaving Disfavored son. It is important to remember that in all these cases, the Auxiliary parent should never withdraw entirely, but rather support the Prime Love-Giver, thereby increasing the PLG's effectiveness.

The Only Child

The circumstances of an only child are quite different from those of children in multiple-sibling families. Since the only child has no siblings with whom to compete, she isn't exposed to the same social or emotional challenges that face children who are raised with siblings. Gone are the day-to-day arguments about personal space and possessions, as well as the constant irritation of having to jostle for every bit of love and privilege that is available.

In most cases, given a competent Prime Love-Giver, an only child will be Favored, since there is no rival brother or sister to take away the PLG's love. As a positive consequence of growing up without siblings, you might expect an only child to be well-behaved and easygoing.

However, there are negative side-effects that result from the lack of competition. An only child may *lack social aggression and be rather poor at defending himself*. By the same token, he may develop a nature that is too kind or too delicate to handle normal adversity.

Another negative possibility is that, because of all the attention that most only children receive, he may become intolerant of other people's intrusion. The only child may get used to peace and quiet, and refuse to bend to the needs of others in terms of time, space, noise, and so on. He may also grow accustomed to being pampered by adults, and as a result become rather spoiled.

A more serious consequence of being an only child is that, since the Circle of Love consists of only two people—the Prime Love-Giving parent and the child—this relationship can easily become very intense, and be the family's central focus of attention. Because of its intensity, there is a risk that the PLG's love may turn into over-protectiveness or smothering. In response, the child could resent all the attention lavished on her, or alternatively, grow guilty at being given so much. In addition, the PLG can become too emotionally dependent on the child. This happens particularly when the Auxiliary Love-Giver is emotionally distant from the family and the Prime Love-Giver has nobody but the lone Favored child to rely on.

Because of the strong bond between a Prime Love-Giver and an only child, another danger lies in *the potential for jealousy on the part of the Auxiliary Love-Giver.* As you will recall, even in multiple-sibling families, the ALG quite frequently becomes jealous of the Favored child. If the only child and the PLG are of the opposite sex, the ALG may become especially envious of their loving relationship. And if the ALG competes with the child for the PLG's love in the same way that a sibling might do, this may make the only child feel out of place in the home.

Finally, just as in the multiple-sibling family, there is always the possibility that the Prime Love-Giver is overanxious or feels inadequate, or that there is some kind of abuse in the life of the only child. In these cases, you would naturally expect problems to arise in the personality of the single child, just as with any other child.

Suicide

The risk of suicide increases dramatically in adolescence, but we still know very little about why this should be so. Family Theory and Favoritism offers some new and plausible explanations for suicide that will hopefully shed more light on these tragedies.

A teenager's motivation for suicide can be the result of being *either* Favored or Disfavored, although suicide is probably more likely if the teenager is feeling Disfavored. As you now know, a Disfavored child feels, rightly or wrongly, rejected by the Prime Love-Giver, and because of this, is filled with a sense of worthlessness. This low self-esteem because she is second best can grow into a deep depression. The Disfavored child feels betrayed by her parents since, as she sees it, they have shown so much more love toward the rival sibling than toward her. She feels she will never measure up to their standards for love. This undermines her self-esteem to such a great extent that she feels there is no purpose left in living, for, as you recall, being connected to the Prime Love-Giver is the child's idea of being connected to life itself. It is these feelings, grown out of control, that form the basis of the attraction of suicide to the Disfavored personality.

In the case of a Favored child, the reasons behind suicide are very different. Favored individuals tend to be extremely sensitive to rejection, and are prone to feelings of guilt and failure. For whatever reasons, the Favored child may feel he has let people down, particularly those who love him most. If the Favored child's sense of pride and self-respect is lost and he becomes humiliated, he may decide he has no recourse but to end his life.

The Favored child may also attempt suicide if he feels displaced and resented at home. This can happen if he feels trapped with a hostile and envious Auxiliary Love-Giver, and perhaps a PLG who is afraid of fully expressing her or his feelings of love to the child. In another scenario, the *Prime Love-Giver* might be deeply depressed. A closely attached Favored child might share this parent's feelings of hopelessness, internalize them as his own, and translate them into the act of suicide.

Abuse

Family Theory and Favoritism gives us a great deal of insight into situations of abuse, as well as the *potential* for abuse in families. It's easy to see, for example, how parental Disfavor could spill over into child abuse, whether physical or emotional. The Disfavored abused child might become the family scapegoat, the one who never does anything right. Naturally, a child will suffer significantly from this kind of treatment.

However, in evaluating family abuse with the help of Family Theory and Favoritism, an inevitable question arises: Who is perpetrating the abuse? Is it the Prime Love-Giver or the Auxiliary Love-Giver? There seems to be no hard-and-fast rule, but since children are mainly guided by the values and feelings of their Prime Love-Giver, *abuse by a Prime Love-Giver will probably do more psychological harm than abuse by an ALG.* Moreover, the effect of abuse by an ALG may be minimized if the children feel protected and shielded by their Prime Love-Giver.

Recent research has suggested that people who suffered abuse as children have a tendency to become abusers themselves in later life. But this broad conclusion hardly seems fair. While it may sometimes be true, it is important to remember that *in many cases, abused children do not grow up to be abusive adults.* Recognizing the psychological closeness between the Prime Love-Giver and the children gives some insight into why this might be so. Using Family Theory and Favoritism, it is important first to find out whether the abusive parent was the Prime or the Auxiliary Love-Giver, and then whether the abused child was Favored or Disfavored. A Favored child who was abused by a detached or alcoholic ALG is *not* likely to become an abuser himself in later years, since his main example for behavior would have come from his Prime Love-Giver. Even a Disfavored child who was abused by an ALG will not necessarily turn out to be abusive since, like the Favored sibling, her main behavioral model also comes from the PLG. However, a Disfavored child will have more trouble putting up with a difficult ALG. He might suffer from personality problems, or even follow in the footsteps of his out-of-control ALG and carry his pent-up rage into his later life with spouse and children.

If the Prime Love-Giver is the abusive parent, this could set a negative role model for all the children. It is worth noting that, especially when there is no other choice, a child may become attached to an abusive Prime Love-Giver. A Favored child who is strongly aligned with an abusive Prime Love-Giver may or may not grow up to inflict the same type of harm on her children. If rejected or made a scapegoat by the abusive PLG, a Disfavored child may also, following this parent's model, abuse others later in life.

But in the final analysis, you should remember that *abusive behavior can surface at any time*, even in a family where neither of the parents was *ever* abused as a child. Especially in cases where alcohol or other chemical agents are involved, abuse can erupt spontaneously, without any examples ever having been set. Similarly, it can end at any time—for example, in the case of a child who becomes severely depressed rather than angry over his treatment.

Like parental abuse, *sibling-to-sibling abuse* can be emotional, physical, or sexual. Cases of physical or sexual abuse of one sibling by another, while rare, are not unheard of. On the other hand, emotional abuse among siblings is quite common and can be found in many so-called normal families where parents don't recognize the viciousness of their children's fighting or simply don't take it seriously enough. As we discussed earlier, parents should keep a close eye on their children's rivalries in order to avoid the kind of severe conflict that can lead to abuse.

As you know, it's more usual for a Disfavored child to be angry at a Favored child, for obvious reasons. However, a Favored child can also abuse a Disfavored sibling, although it is rare. In these cases, the abuse is usually secretly condoned by the PLG, who chooses to ignore it and allow the Favored child to make a scapegoat of the Disfavored one.

Cases of *elder abuse* can be explained in terms of Favoritism too. Anger toward a parent resulting from lifelong feelings of Disfavor may finally find its expression late in life, when the parent is old and weak and the tables are turned. This kind of abuse can be the unfortunate result of placing an elderly parent in the care of a vindictive Disfavored child. Equipped with an understanding of the intense emotional dynamics of Favor and Disfavor, people are able to make better decisions that take into account the bitter feelings among family members that can lead to abuse.

Twins and Siblings Born Very Close Together

What happens when twins are born? Will they *both* be Favored or Disfavored? I touched on this matter when discussing heredity, and cautioned against blaming a child's behavior on his genes.

The truth is that Family Theory and Favoritism principles remain valid with twins, as with any other siblings, since they depend on the basic social instincts that all children possess. *Whether twins are fraternal or identical, they follow exactly the same split pattern of Favor and Disfavor as juxtaposed siblings.* In other words, one twin develops a Favored personality while the other one develops a Disfavored personality.

One minor difference between twins and ordinary siblings is that *twins are more likely to keep their rivalry for each other* rather than joining in rivalries with other older or younger siblings. Even if they do get together with another brother or sister to make a three-sibling cluster of rivals, twins are more likely to band together to offer each other support.

However, in any family, when two children are twins or are born very close to each other, a year apart or thereabouts, one child often becomes the leader while the other is the follower. This behavior—called *the dominance-submission pattern*—can happen between siblings of any age, but it's most likely to occur if the children are close in age or twins. In contrast, *an age difference of eighteen months to two years seems to have the greatest potential for producing intense sibling conflict*. With this age gap, the dominance-submission pattern has a much lower chance of emerging.

A dominance-submission pattern can be a reasonably comfortable solution to the problem of sibling rivalry. As long as neither child is too subdued by the other, siblings involved in a dominance-submission relationship generally develop well and are able to operate peacefully on their own.

Because of this relatively restful atmosphere, in which there appears to be little rivalry or fighting, parents often assume that neither of their children feels Favored or Disfavored, since they hear so few complaints. However, they shouldn't be deceived by their children's outward calm. If the submissive child decides to become more aggressive at some point, parents can expect to see the underlying rivalry suddenly break out. This seems to have been the case with the Friedman twins, better known as Ann Landers and Abigail Van Buren, who got along quite well until a short time after they were married, and then suddenly had a serious falling out.

Dealing With Feelings Of Disfavor as an Adult

After the children of a family grow into adulthood, many still harbour feelings of anger, depression, and anxiety that come from having felt

Disfavored for most of their young lives. How should they deal with these feelings later in life?

As long as parents of adult siblings are still alive—and provided they are willing—there's always the hope that they can someday be moved to change their attitudes toward their Favored and Disfavored children. Balancing their feelings of Favoritism is still the best way to improve both sibling-sibling and parent-child relationships in the family. If parents refuse to change their attitudes toward their children, or are already deceased, the task of resolving sibling conflict becomes more difficult. It remains up to the siblings themselves to try to patch up their differences on their own.

Even when siblings have reached an advanced stage in life, most families still find it beneficial to face up to residual feelings of discontent stemming from Favoritism. There's an undeniable sense of relief that comes from letting go of the past, and especially from saying peaceful good-byes to parents before they die. For many, this alone can be a healing experience.

Both Favored and Disfavored siblings, knowing that life is constantly changing, should always leave the door open for repairing their old relationships. Once people marry and have their own families, they're likely to see things very differently. From a parent's viewpoint, they now experience how difficult it is for parents to mediate between siblings who are competing for their love. They may begin to appreciate the real difficulty their own parents faced in trying to treat them equally.

If sibling strife is carried over into adulthood, everyone will pay a heavy price. First, the rivals lose the privilege of sharing close personal experiences with parents or siblings. Second, their children won't have the opportunity to form close ties with aunts, uncles, cousins, and grandparents. Children who are closely connected with their extended family can benefit enormously from the sense of security and belonging it creates. We recall that children who don't feel they belong to a family group are more likely to be lured away from family values, or to rebel against society. The extended family helps provide this larger group experience. Third, all family members will almost certainly carry a burden of grief for a lifetime.

In most cases, the Family Theory and Favoritism approach can offer a solution to sibling conflict. The starting point is for parents, particularly the Prime Love-Giver, to draw back a little from the Favored child, in order to make room for the Disfavored one. Roseanne Barr's case is a good example. In a public appearance, her mother and sister held hands in an effort to comfort and shield one another from Roseanne's verbal insults. When asked whether she had anything further to tell her family, in her usual abrasive style Roseanne replied that she only regretted not being meaner and ruder toward them. It's easy to figure out that she perceives her sister as a "goody two-shoes" and that she, like any other Disfavored child, is reacting with unbridled anger toward her sister's monopoly of their parents' attention. Unsuspected by her parents—as well as by all those who watch her antics—is Roseanne's deep childhood wish *to be loved more than her younger sister.* Her sensationalist comments are merely a mask—a decoy for her deeply painful, and thoroughly embarrassing, feelings of sadness and low self-esteem.

If a Disfavored child mainly experiences *anger* toward the family, just knowing that this resentment comes from sibling rivalry—one of the most common feelings in life—and that the parents probably would have behaved very differently had they known better, can be a source of comfort. Many Disfavored people recognize that their anger is caused by rivalry with their sibling. But many are not aware of why they feel unhappy, and are in constant search of answers. For example, Phil Donahue always harbored a nagging curiosity about why he got into brutal fights as a child. He never connected his aggressive behavior with the birth of his sister Kathy, whom he considered to be worlds removed. Now, Phil might take comfort in the knowledge that his childhood fear and aggression came mainly from his feelings of anger at the loss of his social position at home, and that, much like Rudolf Dreikurs, he suffered a great loss of self-esteem after his baby sister was born. His anger, it's true, was directed outside the home, but was obviously also combined with a great deal of anxiety and sadness. His combativeness with peers was just a clumsy effort to regain the status that was so suddenly denied him.

Some angry Disfavored siblings show no desire to make amends with their families. Feeling hurt and rejected, they bury their feelings of love for their parents and siblings, and concentrate their efforts on making it on their own. Surprising their families, many break away and set up a much better life for themselves. We remember that Disfavored individuals are typically competitive and shrewd, and value money and the material symbols of success. Many possess both the talents and the sheer dogged drive that it takes to forge ahead of others. Once they are successful, some become the envy of their family of origin, but now they refuse to share their bounty. This is apparently the case with Barbra Streisand, who lives a lavish lifestyle, but gives only a small monthly allowance to her mother and stepsister, Roslyn. We recall that Barbra's troubles increased when her stepfather entered her life. Not only did she lose the primary battle for Favoritism with her older brother Sheldon, but her stepfather always compared her unfavorably with Roslyn. Once he even denied her an ice-cream cone because he said she was too ugly. Roseanne Barr, too, seems to have decided to strike back at her roots. Without a doubt, there are countless people in society with similar stories to tell. From the standpoint of Family Theory and Favoritism, we can understand these acts of retribution as coming from people who, as children and young adults, felt very hurt and ill-used by their families. Our theory passes no moral judgment on their actions, but only tries to explain the reasons behind their choices.

A Disfavored person who does not feel angry, but is mainly depressed and anxious, likely will be constantly battling feelings of pessimism, sadness, fears, or other signs of anxiety such as physical ailments or eating disorders. By adulthood, these ailments and personality traits may have formed deep roots. For the depressed, anxious individual, it's usually helpful to try to *mobilize anger and aggression*. Instead of wallowing in their depression, they should learn to be more demanding of others and more assertive in daily life. For example, the depressed Disfavored person might try some limited therapy in which she takes an *active* rather than a passive role in the treatment. Talking with trusted friends and relatives, becoming involved in community activities, joining assertiveness training groups or public speaking groups—all are useful in alleviating depression and anxiety. Any activities that provide some *feeling of control* over situations and reinforce the individual's self-esteem are worthwhile. Physical activities, such as regular exercise and sports, or intellectual challenges, such as taking courses or debating, are also useful.

If you were a Favored child and you want a truce with your Disfavored sibling, it's best to try to understand of your sibling's resentments and recognize that you'll most likely have to make some concessions. But first, if your Disfavored sibling seems to dislike you no matter what you do, you'll need to ask yourself this question: How far can I trust my Disfavored sibling when she/he resents me so? Unfortunately, some Favored children spend a lifetime battling their envious Disfavored sibling's resentment. If your Disfavored sibling remains adamantly hostile, there's little you can do. Certainly, as a Favored child, you should not relinquish all your rights and self-respect to your Disfavored sibling in the interests of making peace, since your sibling may never be satisfied. For it was mainly up to your parents to equalize their feelings toward the two of you; as a Favored sibling, you're not in a position to repair the damage entirely.

On the other hand, many Disfavored siblings would seize the opportunity to mend the relationship with their Favored sibling, if there were only a little more understanding directed toward them. In these cases, resolving the conflict can be extremely gratifying for everyone.

In the sad situation where parents reject a child's efforts to win their favor, nothing that the Disfavored sibling does may be enough to appease them. In the case of Princess Grace, for example, in spite of all her great achievements, her entire family still treated her like Cinderella whenever they were together. In this unfortunate circumstance, it is best for the Disfavored sibling to try to work through her feelings of disappointment and failure on her own. With or without help, she must somehow come to terms with the idea that, for whatever reasons, her parents never loved her as much as her siblings, and most likely never will. Hers is the task of mourning one of the deepest forms of loss in life.

* * *

The sibling struggle is a universal phenomenon; nobody with siblings can escape it. From the time we're babies until the time we die, Favoritism, as it's played out between a Prime Love-Giving parent and siblings, seems to be the key to the highs and lows of our emotions for a lifetime. Realizing this gives us a great deal more insight into psychology than we have ever had, and in particular, makes human behavior more *predictable* than ever before. Now we can diagnose, explain, and even shape our children's behavior as they grow up. Perhaps our awareness of the impact of Favoritism will make all our futures a little brighter.

Sources

Ainsworth, Mary D. Salter, et. al. *Patterns of Attachment: A Psychological Study of the Strange Situation*. Hillsdale, New Jersey: Wiley, 1978.

Ambrose, Stephen E. *Eisenhower*, vol I. New York: Simon & Schuster, 1985.

Bair, Deirdre. *Simone de Beauvoir: A Biography*. New York: Summit Books, 1990.

Barr, Roseanne. *My Life As a Woman*. New York: Harper & Row, 1989.

Bhatia, Krishan. *Indira: A Biography of Prime Minister Indira Gandhi*. New York: Praeger, 1974.

Bowlby, John. *Attachment and Loss*, vol. 1. London: Hogarth Press, 1969.

Bradford, Sarah. *Princess Grace*. London: Weidenfeld & Nicolson, 1984.

Brendon, Piers. *Winston Churchill: A Brief Life*. Toronto: Stoddart, 1984.

Carr, Virginia Spencer. *The Lonely Hunter: A Biography of Carson McCullers*. Garden City, New York: Doubleday, 1975.

Cathcart, Helen. *The Queen Mother Herself*. London: W.H. Allen, 1979.

Collier, Peter, and David Horowitz. *The Kennedys: An American Drama*. New York: Summit Books, 1984.

Cornwell, Patricia Daniels. *A Time For Remembering: The Story of Ruth Bell Graham*. San Francisco: Harper & Row, 1983.

Daly, Marsha. *Michael Landon: A Biography*. New York: St. Martin's Press, 1987.

Donahue, Phil, & Co. *Donahue: My Own Story*. New York: Simon & Schuster, 1979.

Douglas, Helen Gahagan, June Callwood, ed. *A Full Life*. Garden City, New York: Doubleday, 1982.

Dukakis, Kitty, with Jane Scovell. *Now You Know*. New York: Simon & Schuster, 1990.

Englund, Steven. *Grace of Monaco: An Interpretive Biography*. Garden City, New York: Doubleday, 1984.

Erickson, Carolly. *To the Scaffold: The Life of Marie Antoinette*. New York: William Morrow, 1991.

Faber, Adele, and Elaine Mazlish. *Siblings Without Rivalry: How to Help Your Children Live Together So You Can Live Too*. New York: W.W. Norton, 1987.

Forwood, Margaret. *The Real Benny Hill*. London: Robson Books, 1992.

Fulford, Robert, "The Surprising Side of Northrop Frye." *The Globe and Mail*, July 21, 1993, p. C1.

Furlong, Monica. *Merton: A Biography*. San Francisco: Collins, 1980.

Greene, Nancy, with Jack Batten. *Nancy Greene: An Autobiography*. Don Mills, Ontario: General Publishing, 1968.

Grosskurth, Phyllis. *The Secret Ring: Freud's Inner Circle and the Politics of Psychoanalysis*. Toronto: Macfarlane Walter & Ross, 1991.

Gruber, May. *Pandora's Pride*. Secaucus, New Jersey: L. Stuart, 1984.

Halsey, Margaret. *No Laughing Matter: The Autobiography of a WASP*. Philadelphia: Lippincott, 1977.

Hoffman, Jack, and Daniel Simon. *Run Run Run: The Lives of Abbie Hoffman*. New York: Putnam, 1994.

Kelley, Virginia, with James Morgan. *Leading with My Heart*. New York: Simon & Schuster, 1994.

Lacey, Robert. *Grace*. New York: Putnam, 1994.

Morton, Andrew. *Diana, Her True Story*. London: O'Mara, 1992.

Pavarotti, Luciano, with William Wright. *Pavarotti: My Own Story*. Garden City, New York: Doubleday, 1981.

Pottker, Janice, and Bob Speziale. *Dear Ann, Dear Abby: The Unauthorized Biography of Ann Landers and Abigail Van Buren*. New York: Dodd, Mead, 1987.

Riese, Randall. *Her Name is Barbra: An Intimate Portrait of the Real Barbra Streisand*. Secaucus, New Jersey: Carol Publishing Group, 1993.

Rivers, Joan, with Richard Meryman. *Enter Talking*. New York: Delacorte, 1986.

Smith, Ronald L. *Cosby*. New York: St. Martin's Press, 1986.

Terner, Janet R., and W.L. Pew. *The Courage to be Imperfect: The Life and Work of Rudolf Dreikurs*. New York: Hawthorn, 1978.

Vanderbilt, Gloria. *Once Upon a Time: A True Story*. New York: Knopf, 1985.

Wright, Adrian. *Sylvester Stallone: A Life on Film*. London: Robert Hale, 1991.

Youngs, J. Wm. T. *Eleanor Roosevelt: A Personal and Public Life*. Boston: Little, Brown, 1985.